Green Line 5

Vorschläge zur Leistungsmessung

von
Pauline Ashworth
Katie Hoffman
Carolyn Jones
Stefan Rauschenberg

herausgegeben von
Harald Weisshaar

Ernst Klett Verlag
Stuttgart · Leipzig

Vorwort

Liebe Lehrerin, lieber Lehrer,

die *Green Line 5 Vorschläge zur Leistungsmessung* orientieren sich an den Anforderungen für die Leistungsfeststellung am Gymnasium. Wie Sie wissen, legen aktuelle Lehrpläne Wert auf Kompetenzorientierung und kommunikativen Anspruch. Darauf haben wir bei der Entwicklung dieses Hefts besonderen Wert gelegt, um Ihnen Aufgaben anzubieten, die auf dem neuesten Stand sind und sich daher optimal für die Erstellung von Klassenarbeiten eignen.

Aufbau

Kompetenzbereiche: Pro Unit werden Materialien für Klassenarbeiten zu *Listening, Reading, Writing, Mediation*, Grammatik und Wortschatz sowie *Speaking* angeboten. Die Leistungs-messung in der ausgehenden Mittelstufe soll zunehmend auf die Anforderungen von Testformaten in der gymnasialen Oberstufe vorbereiten. Aus diesem Grund wird in jeder Unit zu jedem der beiden Lesetexte zusätzlich zu den geschlossenen / halboffenen Aufgaben ein Aufgabenapparat angeboten, der die drei Anforderungsbereiche *summary, analysis* und *evaluation* abdeckt. Je nach den Anforderungen Ihres Bundeslandes sind diese Arbeits-aufträge entweder der Kompetenz Lesen oder Schreiben zuzuordnen. Entsprechend den unterschiedlichen Voraussetzungen einiger Bundesländer werden die Aufgaben zur *Grammatik* und zum *Wortschatz* getrennt angeboten. Diese Materialien können somit einfach nach Bedarf eingesetzt werden.
Die Aufgaben sind thematisch nach *Units* gegliedert, und folgen der Progression des Vokabulars im Schülerbuch. Entsprechend der Progression des Schülerbuchs finden Sie nach jeder Unit Aufgabenvorschläge zu den drei *Text smart*-Teilen.

Die beiliegende **CD-ROM** enthält alle Tests und Lösungen als PDF und in editierbarer Form. So können Aufgaben gezielt ausgewählt und die Klassenarbeit individuell zusammengestellt werden. Auf der CD-ROM befinden sich zudem die Audiodateien und Filme (jeweils mit Transkript) zu den Hörverstehen- bzw. Hör- / Sehverstehensaufgaben im Heft. Pro Unit bieten wir Ihnen auf der CD-ROM darüber hinaus einen Vordruck für eine Förderempfehlung an (s. u.).

Die sprachliche Fertigkeit ***Speaking*** kann anhand von drei Schritten getestet werden: *Warm-up* (kurzes L-S Gespräch), *monologue* und *dialogue*. Themenentsprechende *Monologue*- und *Dialogue-Speaking cards* sowie *Teacher's notes* finden Sie im Heft und auf der CD-ROM.

Materialien zur Förderempfehlung

Binnendifferenzierung und individuelle Förderung sind zentrale Bestandteile eines innovativen Fremdsprachenunterrichts, der die Bedürfnisse der einzelnen Schülerinnen und Schüler in den Mittelpunkt rückt und somit zu einem bestmöglichen individuellen Kompetenzaufbau beiträgt. Diese zentralen Bestandteile werden auch in den vorliegenden *Vorschläge zur Leistungsmessung* aufgegriffen. Auf der beiliegenden CD-ROM finden Sie pro Unit eine Förderempfehlung als PDF (für Unit 1 auf S. 3 auch in gedruckter Form) und auch als Word-Datei (editierbar), die es Ihnen ermöglicht, allen SuS, die Förderbedarf aufweisen, eine gezielte Rückmeldung zu diesem zu geben. Die Förderempfehlungen zeigen auf, was die SuS in welchem Kompetenzbereich konkret aufarbeiten und wiederholen müssen, um ihren Förderbedarf auszugleichen. Darüber hinaus erfolgen ausgewählte Querverweise zu passenden Hilfestellungen (bspw. vertiefendes Übungsmaterial) in das Schülerbuch oder Workbook. Dieses Vorgehen ermöglicht nicht nur den Ausgleich des individuellen Förderbedarfs, sondern dient Ihren SuS, deren Eltern und Ihnen auch als Grundlage der Dokumentation des Kompetenzaufbaus und der frühzeitigen Beseitigung von Lernhindernissen. Auf diese Weise erwerben Ihre SuS auch methodische Kompetenzen, erlernen Techniken selbstständigen und eigenverantwortlichen Lernens und nutzen die Förderempfehlungen als *advance organizers* zur Planung und Steuerung ihrer Lernprozesse.

Kommentar zur individuellen Förderung

Name:

Klasse:

Förderempfehlung:
Diese Dinge haben nicht so gut geklappt:

Förderempfehlung	Kompetenzbereich	Ausgewähltes Material zur Vertiefung und Wiederholung
☐ Ich muss noch üben, einem Text, den ich höre, gezielt Informationen zu entnehmen (Schwerpunkt: Gespräch zwischen Jugendlichen / Radiointerview).	Hören	**SB:** S. 24/25, S. 26/1, S. 32/1 **WB:** S. 4/2, S. 6/8
☐ Ich muss noch üben, einem Sachtext / fiktionalen Text, den ich lese, gezielt Informationen zu entnehmen.	Lesen	**SB:** S. 14/1, S. 18/11, S. 20/16, S. 22/21 **WB:** S. 12/20
☐ Ich muss mir noch einmal anschauen und trainieren, wie ich einem Sachtext / fiktionalen Text Informationen entnehmen und auf deren Grundlage eigene Texte verfassen kann: ☐ Zusammenfassung (*summary*) ☐ Analyse der Beziehung von zwei Gruppen zueinander (inkl. passender Beispiele aus dem Text) ☐ Charakterisierung (inkl. passender Beispiele aus dem Text) ☐ *argumentative essay* (Operator: *discuss*) ☐ Artikel (als *comment* mit eigener Meinung) ☐ Tagebucheintrag (*diary entry*)	Lesen / Schreiben	**SB:** S. 31/2–5 **WB:** S. 16/28
☐ Ich muss mir noch einmal anschauen und trainieren, auf der Grundlage vorgegebener Informationen (in Form von Stichpunkten / Bildern) einen Bericht (*report*) / das Script für einen Radiobericht (*radio news report*) zu verfassen.	Schreiben	**SB:** S. 17/10, S. 26/1–2, S. 34/6 **WB:** S. 3/1b, S. 7/10, S. 13/25
☐ Ich muss noch einmal trainieren, wie ich ein Bild beschreiben und Vermutungen über die Hintergründe anstellen / in einer Diskussion mit einem Partner meine Meinung vertreten / zu einer Einigung gelangen kann.	Sprechen	**SB:** S. 12/2, S. 21/19, S. 35/9 **WB:** S. 5/5, S. 11/19
☐ Ich muss noch einmal trainieren, wie ich zielgruppenorientiert eine *informal e-mail* verfassen kann, in der ich gezielt ausgewählte Informationen aus einem deutschsprachigen Sachtext auf Englisch wiedergebe.	Mediation	**SB:** S. 25/28, S. 37/13 **WB:** S. 8/13
☐ Ich muss die Vokabeln aus Unit 1 noch einmal wiederholen: ☐ Wortfeld Australien ☐ Wortfeld safety ☐ synonyms ☐ weiteres Unit-Vokabular	Wortschatz	**SB:** S. 12/1, S. 21/18, S. 36/11 **WB:** S. 3/1, S. 6/7, S. 9/14, S. 11/8
☐ Ich muss die Bildung / die Verwendung des *passive* (inkl. der Verwendung des *by-agent* wiederholen.	Grammatik	**SB:** S. 15/2–4, S. 16/6, S. 17/7–8, S. 19/13, S. 20/17 **WB:** S. 4/3–4, S. 5/6, S. 7/9, S. 8/12
☐ Ich muss die Verwendung von *let, make, allow* und *have* wiederholen.	Grammatik	**SB:** S. 19/14, S. 20/15, S. 35/8 **WB:** S. 7/11
☐ Ich muss die Bildung / die Verwendung der *conditional clauses* wiederholen: ☐ *conditional type I* ☐ *conditional type II* ☐ *conditional type III*	Grammatik	**SB:** S. 23/24, S. 34/7 **WB:** S. 10/15–16
☐ Ich muss die Verwendung von *used to* wiederholen.	Grammatik	**SB:** S. 24/26, S. 33/4 **WB:** S. 11/17

Weitere Anmerkungen:

Ich habe von der Klassenarbeit meines Sohnes/meiner Tochter und von der Förderempfehlung Kenntnis genommen.

_____
(Unterschrift einer/s Erziehungsberechtigten)

Inhalt des Hefts

Vorwort 2

Förderempfehlung (Unit 1) 3

Unit 1 G'day Australia! 5

Text smart 1 A short film 18

Unit 2 The good life? 20

Text smart 2 Informative texts 33

Unit 3 California dreaming 35

Text smart 3 Argumentative texts 48

Solutions 50

Speaking: Teacher's notes 68

Speaking: Bewertungsbogen 72

Unit 1 G'day Australia!

⊙ **1   Listening: Survival training**

You will hear a conversation between Emily, Jake and Lachlan, who are travelling to the outback. Listen to the conversation and answer the questions. You don't have to write complete sentences. You will hear the conversation twice.

1. Why does Emily scream? _____

2. What does Jake want to do? _____

3. What does Lachlan do? _____

4. What should they do if they are bitten by a spider or a snake?

    _____

5. How many people are bitten by spiders every year? _____

6. How many people have died from spider and snake bites in the last fifty years?

    _____

7. How does Jake feel when he hears this information? _____

8. What are they going to do when they've set up camp? _____

9. Where are they going to get their food and water from?

    _____

10. How long have Jake and Emily been in Australia? _____

11. Where is Jake spending the most time on his holiday? _____

12. How long is Jake going to stay in Australia? _____

Green Line 5
Vorschläge zur Leistungsmessung
ISBN: 978-3-12-834254-2
Textquellen: Pauline Ashworth, Stuttgart
Illustratorin: Simone Pahl, Berlin

⊙ **2   Listening: A big hole**

Read the questions and answers below. Then listen to the radio interview with Madeleine Collard. Choose the correct answer or answers. You will hear this interview twice.

1. What was happening when the police arrived at the camp?

   a) ☐ The children were eating dinner.
   b) ☐ The women were making dinner.
   c) ☐ The men were fixing buildings at the camp.

2. Why was Madeleine's mum so upset when she saw the police?

   a) ☐ She was scared of the police because they had taken her away when she was young.
   b) ☐ She probably knew that the police sometimes took children away from their Aboriginal parents.
   c) ☐ The police had looked for her as soon as they arrived in the camp.

3. Where was Madeleine's father?

   a) ☐ Madeleine never knew exactly where her father was.
   b) ☐ He was probably working somewhere else.
   c) ☐ He was looking for food for them to eat.

4. Where had Madeleine's ancestors lived?

   a) ☐ They had moved from place to place as they wanted to.
   b) ☐ They had lived in a settlement in a different part of the land.
   c) ☐ They had been moved from one camp to another.

5. Why were Madeleine and her relatives living in a camp?

   a) ☐ Because they could stay safer in the camp away from the dangers of the outback.
   b) ☐ Because they could no longer find enough food as their ancestors had done.
   c) ☐ Because their own land had been stolen.

6. When did Madeleine meet her new parents?

   a) ☐ When the police took her to the children's home.
   b) ☐ After her new foster parents had paid for her.
   c) ☐ When she was taken to their house.

7. What did Madeleine's new parents give her?

   a) ☐ toys, clothes and food
   b) ☐ a home and culture
   c) ☐ love and freedom of choice

8. What did Madeleine think about her foster parents?

   a) ☐ They treated her well but they never really cared for her.
   b) ☐ They gave her everything but she still felt like something was missing.
   c) ☐ They made her happy because they treated her well and she loved them.

9. Why did Madeleine always feel lonely?

   a) ☐ Because she felt as though nobody loved her or cared for her.
   b) ☐ Because she couldn't make friends among the white people she lived with.
   c) ☐ Because she felt as though she really belonged to the land and her original people.

Klett
Green Line 5
Vorschläge zur Leistungsmessung
ISBN: 978-3-12-834254-2

© Ernst Klett Verlag GmbH, Stuttgart 2018 | www.klett.de
Von dieser Druckvorlage ist die Vervielfältigung für den eigenen
Unterrichtsgebrauch gestattet. Die Kopiergebühren sind
abgegolten. Alle Rechte vorbehalten.

Textquellen: Pauline Ashworth, Stuttgart

3 Reading: A newspaper article

Australian dig finds evidence of Aboriginal habitation up to 80,000 years ago

by Helen Davidson at Madjedbebe and Calla Wahlquist | 19 July 2017

Artefacts in Kakadu national park have been dated between 65,000 and 80,000 years old, extending[1] likely occupation[2] of area by thousands of years

A groundbreaking[3] archaeological discovery in Australia's north has extended the known length of time Aboriginal people have inhabited[4] the continent to at least 65,000 years.

5 The findings on about 11,000 artefacts from Kakadu national park, published on Thursday in the journal *Nature*, prove Indigenous people have been in Australia for far longer than the much-contested[5] estimates of between 47,000 and 60,000 years, the researchers said. Some of the artefacts were potentially[6] as old as 80,000 years.

"People got here much earlier than we thought, which means of course they must also have left
10 Africa much earlier to have traveled on their long journey through Asia and south-east Asia to Australia," said the lead author, Associate Prof Chris Clarkson, from the University of Queensland.

The site at Madjedbebe is on the traditional lands of the Mirarr people, but currently[7] within the confines[8] of the Jabiluka uranium mining lease[9], and surrounded by the 20,000 hectares of the heritage[10]-listed Kakadu.

15 "We'd like to tell people we were here long enough – tell all the Balanda [non-Indigenous people] about the stories, that people were here a long time," Mirarr traditional owner May Nango said.

Under the agreement, which Clarkson described as one of the strongest in Australia, the Mirarr have total control over the extent[11] of the dig, and veto power. All discoveries must be reported to them and all artefacts must be returned to the Mirarr at the end of the project.
20 "They have to bring it back here, it belongs to this place," said May Nango, a Mirarr traditional owner. "We trust them to work this place."
Nango said the country had to be protected for the younger generations, and she was worried about non-Indigenous people coming in and clearing out trees or mining.
"We like to stay forever, we're buried[12] here too. We like to stay forever on our land, and we like to
25 teach our young kids too so they remember our old people who gave us the stories."

Source: www.theguardian.com (abridged)

1 **extend** verlängern | 2 **occupation** hier: Besiedlung | 3 **groundbreaking** bahnbrechend |
4 **inhabit** bewohnen | 5 **much-contested** sehr umstritten | 6 **potentially** möglicherweise |
7 **currently** derzeit | 8 **confines** Grenzen | 9 **uranium mining lease** Pachtvertrag für den Uranabbau |
10 **heritage** Kulturerbe | 11 **extent** Ausmaß | 12 **bury** begraben

Green Line 5
Vorschläge zur Leistungsmessung
ISBN: 978-3-12-834254-2

© Ernst Klett Verlag GmbH, Stuttgart 2018 | www.klett.de
Von dieser Druckvorlage ist die Vervielfältigung für den eigenen
Unterrichtsgebrauch gestattet. Die Kopiergebühren sind
abgegolten. Alle Rechte vorbehalten.

Textquellen: *Australian dig finds evidence of Aboriginal habitation up to
80,000 years ago* by Helen Davidson, The Guardian, July 19, 2017
Illustratorin: Simone Pahl, Berlin

Comprehension

Read the text and answer the questions with short answers.

1. How old are the objects which have recently been found in the Kakadu National Park?

   _____

2. Who made these objects? _____

3. Why are these old objects so important? _____

   _____

4. Where were the results of the research published? _____

5. Why is Africa mentioned in the article? _____

   _____

6. Why is one indigenous Australian pleased about the findings? _____

   _____

7. Who can decide when the work should be stopped? _____

8. What will happen to anything which is found on Mirarr people's land? _____

   _____

9. What is May Nango worried about? (two items)? _____

   _____

10. What is important to the Mirarr people? (3 items) _____

   _____

Comprehension – Analysis – Evaluation

a) *Summarise what the text tells you about the scientific discoveries made in Madjedbebe in less than 100 words.*

b) *The relationship between the Balandas and Aboriginal people has changed over the last couple of hundred years. Analyse the relationship now using examples from the text.*

c) *Discuss whether you think it's good that indigenous people own the land at Madjedbebe and have the right to decide about it or if you think this land should belong to all Australians.*

   Or

   Write an article in which you give your opinion on the fact that all the historical artefacts must be given back to the Mirarr people.

Green Line 5
Vorschläge zur Leistungsmessung
ISBN: 978-3-12-834254-2

© Ernst Klett Verlag GmbH, Stuttgart 2018 | www.klett.de
Von dieser Druckvorlage ist die Vervielfältigung für den eigenen
Unterrichtsgebrauch gestattet. Die Kopiergebühren sind
abgegolten. Alle Rechte vorbehalten.

Textquellen: Pauline Ashworth, Stuttgart

4 Reading: Angela

by James Moloney

Angela and Gracey were going to be "best friends forever" but after they had made it into the same university, Gracey's Aboriginal heritage started to develop a new meaning.

5 *As neither of them had much money, they were both very happy to be able to live with Angela's parents … at first. Angela is driving them both home from university when they have the following conversation.*

10 "All right," I said in mock exasperation. "Out with it."
"OK, OK! It's Shirley. Do you remember her from that day in the Great Court?"
"Not really."
15 "It was her party I went to. She shares that big old house with two other Murri[1] girls. There was a fourth but she left at the end of last week."
Still I didn't suspect[2], even though Gracey
20 paused and took a quick look at my face, as though she was waiting for me to guess. "They've asked me to move in."
I nearly drove us in the river. "Move in? But what about …" I managed to stop in time. To be honest, I was going to say "what about 25
me", because that was the first thought that came into my head.
"Do you mind, Angela?" she asked sheepishly. "If you don't want me to, I'll say no. I have to tell them by Friday so they can 30
look for someone else. Money's pretty tight[3] and they need an extra person to share the rent."
"It's your decision, I suppose." What a weak thing to say. The truth was, I was too stunned 35
to work out what I really thought.
"Yeah, I know it's my decision but I wanted to talk it through with you and Cheryl[4]."
"I thought you were happy living with us. You know, sisters." 40
"I am, but … It's being round other black kids. Ever since I went to the Unit[5], I've felt so much better about being here. It's probably hard for you to understand, Angela. You've never lived amongst people different from 45
you, and it's not just the way I look, my skin colour. It's feeling at home, being with people who pick up the same things as me, little things like being looked at in the refec[6] and having lecturers[7] worried you won't be able to 50
keep up."
"I thought you didn't notice things like that anymore."
"You always notice, Angela. It's just a question of whether you care or not. Trouble 55
is, I got used to being the only one. Now I'm not alone anymore."

Source: James Moloney, 'Angela' (abridged and adapted)

---

1 **Murri** *Bezeichnung, die Aborigines für sich selbst verwenden, v.a. in New South Wales und Victoria* |
2 **suspect** *ahnen* | 3 **tight** *hier: knapp* | 4 *Cheryl ist Angelas Mutter* | 5 **the Unit** *(kurz für "Indigenous Student Support Unit") eine Studentengruppe für Aborigines* | 6 **refec** *(kurz für „refectory") Mensa* |
7 **lecturer** *Dozent*

Green Line 5
Vorschläge zur Leistungsmessung
ISBN: 978-3-12-834254-2

© Ernst Klett Verlag GmbH, Stuttgart 2018 | www.klett.de
Von dieser Druckvorlage ist die Vervielfältigung für den eigenen
Unterrichtsgebrauch gestattet. Die Kopiergebühren sind
abgegolten. Alle Rechte vorbehalten.

Textquellen: Pauline Ashworth, Stuttgart; *Angela* by James Moloney, first
published by University of Queensland Press, 1998
Bildquellen: Klett-Archiv

Comprehension

Read the text and then the statements. Tick ✓ true or false and give the line numbers where you can find the information.

	true	false	line(s)
1. Angela and Gracey have both left school and have just started to study.			
2. Shirley is a white Australian who Gracey met at a party.			
3. Gracey thinks Angela might already know what she wants to talk to her about.			
4. Gracey has asked Shirley if she can move into her house.			
5. Angela is surprised that Gracey wants to share a house with other girls because she doesn't have much money.			
6. Gracey won't move out if Angela doesn't want her to.			
7. Shirley and her friends own the house, but it's still expensive to live there.			
8. Gracey wants to move out of Angela's house because she wants to live with people who have had the same experience as she has had.			
9. Until now Angela has lived with other white Australians.			
10. People have always treated Gracey differently because she's black.			
11. Angela didn't know that Gracey has suffered discrimination.			
12. Gracey had felt lonely before she met other Aboriginal girls.			

Comprehension – Analysis – Evaluation

a) *In less than 100 words, outline Gracey's reasons why she wants to move out.*

b) *Give a character description of Angela and Gracey, and then analyse their relationship using examples from the text.*

c) *Gracey writes a diary every day. Write her diary entry on the evening after her discussion with Angela.*

Or

Discuss whether the situation would be different if both Gracey and Angela were black or white, and why / why not.

Green Line 5
Vorschläge zur Leistungsmessung
ISBN: 978-3-12-834254-2

© Ernst Klett Verlag GmbH, Stuttgart 2018 | www.klett.de
Von dieser Druckvorlage ist die Vervielfältigung für den eigenen
Unterrichtsgebrauch gestattet. Die Kopiergebühren sind
abgegolten. Alle Rechte vorbehalten.

Textquellen: Pauline Ashworth, Stuttgart

5 Writing: A report about your exchange program

During the winter holidays you went to Australia on an exchange program. You are asked to write a report about the trip for the organisation.

Your program may help you to remember the details of your trip:

WELCOME to Australia!	
Here is the program for our trip activities and events:	
23th December	Flight to Sydney
24th December	Relax in youth hostel and visit Sydney Harbour
25th December	Christmas party on Bondi Beach
27th December	Exploring Sydney (Sydney Opera House, Sydney Harbour Bridge, Museum of Sydney)
28th December – 4th January	The Outback Experience with a guide, including: – walking tours through the outback – learning about Australian wildlife – meeting with Aborigines – presentation and discussion about the Stolen Generation
5th – 10th January	Experience school life in an Australian school

6 Writing: A radio news report

Look at the pictures and write the script for a radio news report about what happened.

Green Line 5
Vorschläge zur Leistungsmessung
ISBN: 978-3-12-834254-2

© Ernst Klett Verlag GmbH, Stuttgart 2018 | www.klett.de
Von dieser Druckvorlage ist die Vervielfältigung für den eigenen
Unterrichtsgebrauch gestattet. Die Kopiergebühren sind
abgegolten. Alle Rechte vorbehalten.

Textquellen: Pauline Ashworth, Stuttgart
Illustratorin: Simone Pahl, Berlin

7 Mediation: Travelling in Australia

You're going to Sydney to visit an aunt with a British cousin. The two of you would like to travel around together. First choose one of the pictures – this is your cousin. Then use the picture and the information about him or her to imagine what he/she is like. Write an e-mail to him/her and say which places you should visit. Give reasons.

 James: 18 years; likes cities; enjoys shopping and doing sports at the studio or at the beach; often goes surfing; loves riding his motocross

 Sienna: 18 years; sings in a band; doesn't enjoy sports; likes to relax in the outdoors; interested in nature (wants to study Biology)

Australiens Ostküste

Aus dem Dschungel in den Dschungel

Im RTL-Dschungelcamp geht es um Gestrüpp, Urwald und gefährliches Getier. Aber an der Ostküste Australiens warten weitaus attraktivere Ziele. Wir hätten da ein paar Vorschläge.
Von Carolin Gasteiger

Noosa

Das beschauliche Noosa liegt etwa 120 Kilometer nördlich von Brisbane und ist zweigeteilt. In Noosaville locken schicke Restaurants und Cafés, in Noosa Heads geht es am Strand entlang durch den Nationalpark. Surfer können sich hier in die Wellen stürzen, ganz ohne den Trubel im überlaufenen Partyort Surfers Paradise. Aber wundern Sie sich nicht, wenn ein Einheimischer auf dem Brett neben Ihnen einen Kopfstand macht. Ganz in der Nähe von Noosa liegt außerdem der Australia Zoo. Bekannt gemacht hat ihn der „Krokodiljäger" Steve Irwin, der 2006 bei einem Tauchunfall ums Leben kam.

Lamington National Park

An Nationalparks mangelt es Australien nicht. Im fast 100 Jahre alten Lamington National Park im Südosten des Bundesstaates Queensland können Besucher den größten subtropischen Urwald Australiens entdecken. Auf den mehr als 200 Quadratkilometern des Unesco-Weltnaturerbes warten dichter Regenwald, uralte Bäume und mehr als 500 Wasserfälle auf Besucher.

Agnes Water/1770

An den zwei benachbarten Dörfern fahren viele auf dem Weg nach Norden vorbei. Tatsächlich gibt es hier weder Sehenswürdigkeiten noch ausgeprägtes Nachtleben. Auf einer Chopper die Küstenstraße entlang zu fahren zählt hier zu den Highlights. Die Reisenden, die bleiben, teilen sich auf drei Hostels auf. Trotzdem ist Agnes Water/1770 ideal für alle, die sich vor den Touristenmassen am Great Barrier Reef ein paar Tage Auszeit gönnen wollen. Und es ist einer der letzten Orte an der Ostküste, an denen Surfen noch möglich ist, bevor das Riff den Wellengang stoppt.

Whitsunday Islands

Ein Segeltörn von Airlie Beach zu den Whitsunday Islands gehört für viele Australienurlauber zum Programm. James Cook entdeckte die Inselgruppe an Pfingsten 1770 und gab ihnen damit ihren Namen: Pfingstinseln. Neben Hamilton Island und der größten Insel, Whitsunday Island, lohnt sich ein Abstecher zum Whitehaven Beach mit seinem schneeweißen Sand. Wem es auf einem Boot zu wackelig ist: Von Airlie Beach aus fliegen auch Helikopter oder Wasserflugzeuge über das Archipel. Zwischen Mai und September können auch Buckelwale vorbeikommen.

Source: www.sueddeutsche.de

Klett

Green Line 5
Vorschläge zur Leistungsmessung
ISBN: 978-3-12-834254-2

© Ernst Klett Verlag GmbH, Stuttgart 2018 | www.klett.de
Von dieser Druckvorlage ist die Vervielfältigung für den eigenen
Unterrichtsgebrauch gestattet. Die Kopiergebühren sind
abgegolten. Alle Rechte vorbehalten.

Textquellen: Pauline Ashworth, Stuttgart; *Australiens Ostküste: Aus dem Dschungel in den Dschungel* by Carolin Gasteiger, Sueddeutsche Zeitung, February 1, 2014
Bildquellen: shutterstock (iko), New York, NY; shutterstock (sergey causelove), New York, NY

8   Vocabulary: Safety in the outback → (after Station 1)

Write the word or phrase which is missing from the safety advice.

1. When you go bushwalking, always go in a group.

   Don't go off _____.

2. Always wear boots and walk loudly. Most snakes

   aren't aggressive and aren't _____ to bite

   you if they hear you coming.

3. Don't panic! And remember that most bites are not _____ if you get help in time.

4. Make sure that you have a _____ phone with you. Normal mobile phones don't work

   in the outback.

5. And use your phone if you are unsure! Don't worry that you will _____ somebody.

   Air ambulance crews are happy to be called out.

6. Your _____ comes first. If you have been bitten, get it treated. And fast.

7. Don't leave _____. Always take everything with you, especially paper and bottles.

   They can cause bushfires.

8. Don't _____ and eat fruit if you don't know that it's OK for you to eat. You don't want

   to be sick in the outback.

9   Vocabulary: My family → (after Station 2)

Find synonyms for the words underlined in these sentences.

1. My dad loves his job as a teacher. – _____

2. He says he's always surprised at the cultural variety of people he meets every day. –

   _____

3. He meets lots of people from abroad. – _____

4. They say he's quite good at teaching. – _____

5. But he also likes to fix things around the school. – _____

6. A lot of my aunts, uncles and cousins are teachers too. – _____

Textquellen: Pauline Ashworth, Stuttgart
Bildquellen: Klett-Archiv (Lothar Rother, Schwäbisch Gmünd), Stuttgart

10   Vocabulary: Australia Day → (after Station 3)

Read the letter to the newspaper and underline the correct words.

Dear Sir,

Once again it's almost Australia Day. Many people will celebrate, but others, like many of our friends and relatives, always go to protect / protest / prove at what they describe as this totally disrespectful / nonrespectful / unrespectful holiday – which celebrates the beginning of the end of life as we knew it for all Aborigines. Instead of protesting, my family and I will do our yearly walkabout, where we walk to remember the thousands of years we could live freely as elders / nomads / seniors, going where we wanted, when we wanted – the time before the first ships with English convicts / tourists / travellers arrived on 26th January 1788. We want to celebrate the dreaming / knowing / knowledge that all indigenous people had and still have of our beautiful country. I want to forget my childhood / children / elders, when I was taken away from my parents and given to a foster family. On this special ancestor / anniversary / birthday, 50 years since Aborigines were first counted as Australians, my family and I want to be further away from the Australia Day celebration than ever, and we want you to know why.

11   Language: Invitations → (after Station 1)

Complete the dialogue with the correct form of the passive.

Amy: _____ (you; invite) to Pete's party on Saturday? Pete's going to

have it on the beach after the surfing competition.

Jade: Yes, but I can't go. I_____ (just; ask) to visit Yang's house in

Brisbane when I _____ (give) the invitation. _____ the

competition _____ (hold) in any weather? There are no waves at the moment.

Amy: Oh, yes, it _____ (always; organise) for the second weekend of

September but there are always lots of waves; don't worry.

It_____ (show) all over the world and there'll be lots of famous

names there, like that Mick Fanning.

Jade: The one who _____ almost _____ (bite) by a shark during a competition?

Amy: Yes, but don't worry. That won't happen here in Sydney. I think the bay

_____ even _____ (protect) by lifeguards on motor boats.

Green Line 5
Vorschläge zur Leistungsmessung
ISBN: 978-3-12-834254-2

© Ernst Klett Verlag GmbH, Stuttgart 2018 | www.klett.de
Von dieser Druckvorlage ist die Vervielfältigung für den eigenen
Unterrichtsgebrauch gestattet. Die Kopiergebühren sind
abgegolten. Alle Rechte vorbehalten.

Textquellen: Pauline Ashworth, Stuttgart

12 Language: Taronga Zoo → (after Station 1)

Rewrite the underlined sentences in the correct form of the passive. Decide if you need the by-agent or not.

Taronga is Sydney's city zoo, and as <u>they built it at Sydney Harbour</u>, it lives up to its name, Taronga, which means "beautiful view" in an Aboriginal language. <u>Albert Le Souef had suggested the location</u> because there was lots of space for the animals there. One hundred years later <u>the zoo still protects wildlife</u> for future generations. Today <u>you can see over 4,000 animals</u> at the zoo.

Many of our animals are from Australia and the most local are from Sydney itself: little penguins. These are the smallest species of penguin and <u>we must protect them</u> as they are in danger of extinction. As they live near the city centre, <u>dogs often attack these penguins</u>. When possible <u>we treat these penguins</u> until they are healthy again and then <u>we set them free in the wild</u>.
<u>You can reach the zoo by ferry</u> within 12 minutes from the city centre, and there's so much to do and see that you can easily spend the day here.

13 Language: New Year now and then → (after Station 2)

Andy, an Australian exchange student from Sydney, is writing a blog about his Christmas experiences in Germany. Write the underlined sentences again in the passive form.

Yesterday I had my first visit to a Christmas market in Germany. <u>My friends and I got there early the first morning, so the people were still hanging up a few decorations and were doing some other last minute preparations.</u> <u>I was surprised by all the different kinds of things that people were selling</u> – I saw not just food, decorations and artwork (like you find at our Christmas markets) but everything from clothes to cooking tools to cleaning products! <u>While someone was showing us some special kitchen knives, one of my friends went to get us all her favourite Christmas food</u> – Bratwurst! It was strange for me to eat sausage at a Christmas market, but it tasted great! Today my friends and I are at another Christmas market that is even bigger than the one yesterday. <u>All around me children and adults are performing all sorts of traditional Christmas songs.</u> <u>People are eating sweet nuts and drinking Christmas punch</u> – the mood here is fantastic! It's fun to watch the crowd. A group of kids are about to go skating at the outdoor ice rink here, but I heard them say that none of them know how to skate! <u>The man is still giving them the skates and is telling them to be careful</u>, but they aren't afraid. Let's see how well they do!

Green Line 5
Vorschläge zur Leistungsmessung
ISBN: 978-3-12-834254-2

© Ernst Klett Verlag GmbH, Stuttgart 2018 | www.klett.de
Von dieser Druckvorlage ist die Vervielfältigung für den eigenen
Unterrichtsgebrauch gestattet. Die Kopiergebühren sind
abgegolten. Alle Rechte vorbehalten.

Textquellen: Pauline Ashworth, Stuttgart
Bildquellen: shutterstock (Constantin Stanciu), New York, NY; shutterstock
(Ian Law); New York, NY; shutterstock (stockvideoshooter), New York, NY

14   Language: January on the beach → (after Station 2)

*Read the short dialogues and then complete the sentence using: **let**, **make**, **allow** or **have**.*

Sarah:	Yes, Mum. I'm still on the beach, but Jake's just cutting my hair. I'll be home in an hour.	Sarah is _____ _____ .
Chang:	So are you coming to my party on the 20th?	Peter's parents _____
Peter:	Yes, my parents have said that I could stay another week.	_____ .
Lifeguard:	Where do you think you are all going? You must clean up that litter before you go.	The lifeguard _____
Fiona:	Oh, I'm very sorry about that.	_____ .
Lizzie:	Oh, please let me go surfing. I'm old enough now.	Lizzie's mum _____
Mum:	OK, you can go, but don't go too far out.	_____ .
Mum:	No, Lizzie. You must wear your T-shirt. The sun is too strong at this time of year.	Lizzie's mum _____ _____ .
Pam:	Look at him. He's a really famous surfer. Will you take a photo of me talking to him?	Pam wants _____ _____ .

15   Language: An exchange trip to Sydney → (after Station 2)

Write the sentences again in the passive.

1. The English teachers at our school offered the students a trip to Sydney.

_____

2. It was an exchange trip and our partners sent us letters about themselves and their families.

_____ Australian partners and their families.

3. When we arrived in Australia the families showed us Sydney.

_____ when we arrived there.

4. My new friend taught me some surfing tricks.

_____

5. Jacob's host family gave Jacob a new surfboard.

_____

6. The teachers had promised us a great experience before we left home and they weren't wrong.

_____ before we left home.

Green Line 5
Vorschläge zur Leistungsmessung
ISBN: 978-3-12-834254-2
Textquellen: Pauline Ashworth, Stuttgart

16 Language: Car problems in the outback! → (after Station 3)

Jake and his sister Chloe are taking a trip to the outback when their car breaks down … Make conditional sentences type 1, 2 or 3 that have the same meaning as the given sentence(s).

Chloe: Dad should have lent me his car. His car wouldn't have broken down.

_____

Jake: There's no signal for our mobiles. We can't call anybody because our mobiles don't work.

_____

Chloe: We must go and look for water soon or we'll die of thirst.

_____

Jake: No, we can't do that. We mustn't leave the car because then nobody will find us again.

_____

Chloe: Nobody has found us because we didn't stay on the main road.

_____

17 Language: Moving to the outback → (after Station 3)

*Alinta has moved to the outback from Sydney. Compare her life in the outback today with how it used to be in Sydney. Use **used to** or **didn't use to** plus the correct verb in the box.*

| go | have | meet | be | think | worry | walk | buy |

When we lived in Sydney, we _____ to the beach almost every day. In Sydney

we _____ about water, but here on our farm we can't even go swimming because

there's not enough water to fill a pool. We _____ what we wanted any time, but now

we're a long way from any shops. In Sydney we _____ about it – the shops were so

near, we could just go shopping again. The biggest change for us is that we _____ to

school, but now we do our lessons at home mostly on a computer and a teacher visits us about

once a month. We _____ our friends at school, but now we mostly chat online. It isn't

as bad as it sounds though. We _____ as much time in Sydney, because we always

had lots of homework. And we _____ bored by teachers talking for hours, but now we

can just turn them off. ☺

Green Line 5
Vorschläge zur Leistungsmessung
ISBN: 978-3-12-834254-2

© Ernst Klett Verlag GmbH, Stuttgart 2018 | www.klett.de
Von dieser Druckvorlage ist die Vervielfältigung für den eigenen
Unterrichtsgebrauch gestattet. Die Kopiergebühren sind
abgegolten. Alle Rechte vorbehalten.

Textquellen: Pauline Ashworth, Stuttgart

17

Text smart 1 A short film

1   The plot

Watch Clip 2 (03:04 minutes) from the short film 'A Great Mistake'. Remember to listen carefully too. Then answer the questions with short answers.

1. What does Greg do at the beginning of the film? _____

2. What do the police say when they arrest him? (2 items) _____

   _____

3. What reason does he give for his behavior? _____

4. Why has Greg been arrested apart from trespassing on private property? _____

   _____

5. What is Greg's reaction to this message? _____

6. What happens when he is alone in the room? _____

   _____

7. What is the time and place of the meeting? _____

2   Getting from picture A to picture B

Greg is locked up in an interrogation room at a police station with a police officer watching him. A moment later, he is out of that room and wearing a police uniform. How did that happen? Tick ✓ the correct answer and give the reason why you think your answer is right.

a) ☐ Greg and the police officer are friends and the police officer lent Greg a uniform.
b) ☐ Greg punched the police officer and then stole his uniform.
c) ☐ The police officer lets him borrow it.

Reason: _____

Annotations:
1 **trespassing** unerlaubtes Betreten │ 2 **private property** Privatgrundstück │ 3 **suspect** Verdächtiger │
4 **missing person case** Vermisstenfall │ 5 **interrogation room** Verhörraum

Green Line 5
Vorschläge zur Leistungsmessung
ISBN: 978-3-12-834254-2

© Ernst Klett Verlag GmbH, Stuttgart 2018 | www.klett.de
Von dieser Druckvorlage ist die Vervielfältigung für den eigenen
Unterrichtsgebrauch gestattet. Die Kopiergebühren sind
abgegolten. Alle Rechte vorbehalten.

Textquellen: Gerlind Becker, Berlin
Bildquellen: February Films, London

3 The setting

Look at the film stills below. Where does the action take place? Describe the settings.

4 The genre and its key elements

What is the genre of the film clip? How do you know? Name at least six key elements.

5 Body language and facial expressions

Look at the film stills. Describe the characters' body language and facial expressions, using adjectives that express their emotions. Explain why the characters are feeling the way they do.

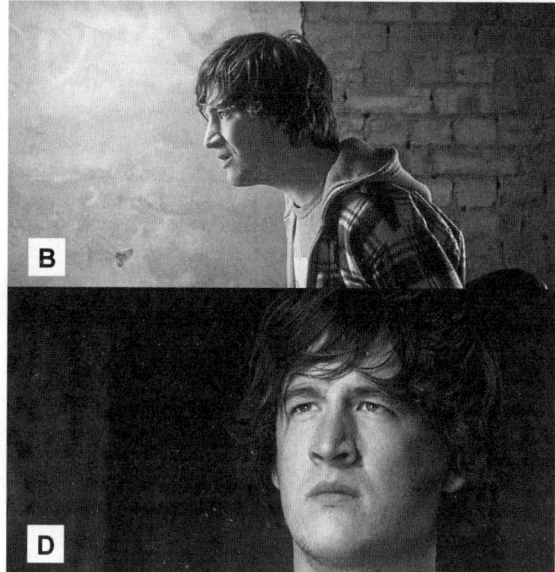

6 Shot sizes

What shot sizes (close-up, medium, wide) are used here? Why do you think these were chosen?

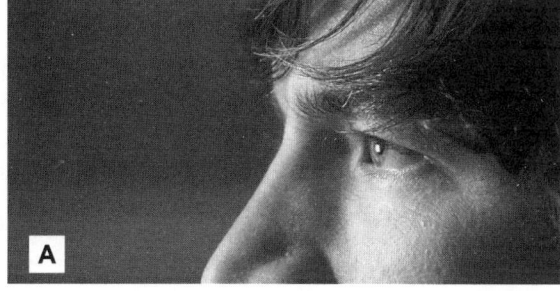

Green Line 5
Vorschläge zur Leistungsmessung
ISBN: 978-3-12-834254-2

© Ernst Klett Verlag GmbH, Stuttgart 2018 | www.klett.de
Von dieser Druckvorlage ist die Vervielfältigung für den eigenen
Unterrichtsgebrauch gestattet. Die Kopiergebühren sind
abgegolten. Alle Rechte vorbehalten.

Textquellen: Gerlind Becker, Berlin
Bildquellen: February Films, London

Unit 2 The good life?

◉ **1 Listening: An unusual life**

Listen to a radio interview with a teenage boy who has had an unusual life. Choose the correct answer(s). There can be more than one correct answer.

1. The families in the documentary had moved to places which …

   a) ☐ were far away.

   b) ☐ had more job opportunities.

   c) ☐ had better homes.

2. Why did the presenter think the children might not be happy?

   a) ☐ The places were far away from everything.

   b) ☐ Children don't like change.

   c) ☐ It wasn't their idea to move.

3. Since the documentary was shown, Josh has …

   a) ☐ gone to Australia.

   b) ☐ visited his grandparents.

   c) ☐ left his family.

4. How did Josh's parents' way of life in London make the parents feel?

   a) ☐ bored

   b) ☐ stressed

   c) ☐ too busy

5. What does Josh remember about the photos his parents showed him?

   a) ☐ the water

   b) ☐ the colours

   c) ☐ the buildings

6. At first, how did Josh feel about the idea of living on an island?

   a) ☐ It sounded perfect.

   b) ☐ He would miss his school.

   c) ☐ It would be hard to survive.

7. What kind of education did Josh's parents offer him?

   a) ☐ They would teach him themselves.

   b) ☐ He would teach himself.

   c) ☐ He would go to a local school.

8. On the island, Josh says he couldn't …

   a) ☐ be with kids as old as he was.

   b) ☐ make friends.

   c) ☐ enjoy life.

9. Josh's parents …

   a) ☐ prepared him well for his exams.

   b) ☐ didn't believe in qualifications.

   c) ☐ could teach a variety of things.

10. What does Josh hope for his brothers?

   a) ☐ They will leave the island too.

   b) ☐ They will move to a different island.

   c) ☐ They will stay with their parents.

Klett

Green Line 5
Vorschläge zur Leistungsmessung
ISBN: 978-3-12-834254-2

© Ernst Klett Verlag GmbH, Stuttgart 2018 | www.klett.de
Von dieser Druckvorlage ist die Vervielfältigung für den eigenen
Unterrichtsgebrauch gestattet. Die Kopiergebühren sind
abgegolten. Alle Rechte vorbehalten.

Textquellen: Carolyn Jones, Beckenham
Bildquellen: Fotolia.com (Natalia Lysenko), New York

2 Listening: Can I really do that job?

Jim and Chloe are talking about the career talks they have just heard. Listen[1] and complete the table with the correct information from the text.

	Jim	Chloe
What was the profession of the visitor who spoke to Jim/Chloe's group?		
What did Jim/Chloe think about the profession before they heard the talk?		
What did Jim/Chloe learn about the jobs? Name 2 things for Jim and 3 things for Chloe.	1. 2.	1. 2. 3.
Will Jim/Chloe consider doing the profession? Why/Why not?		

1 **ballet** ['bæleɪ] Ballett

Textquellen: Carolyn Jones, Beckenham
Bildquellen: shutterstock (Monkey Business Images), New York, NY

3 Reading: About a Boy

'About a Boy', by Nick Hornby, is about a 36-year old man called Will Freeman, who is single, child-free and lives the life of a teenager. He doesn't have to work because his father once wrote a Christmas song which made him and his family very rich. When Will meets 12-year-old Marcus and his mother, his life changes dramatically.

5 Filling days had never really been a problem for Will. He might not have been proud of his lifelong lack of[1] achievement, but he was proud of his ability to keep himself above water in the huge ocean of time he had at his disposal[2]; a less resourceful[3] man, he felt, might have gone under and drowned.

The evenings were fine; he knew people. He didn't know how he knew them, because he'd never
10 had colleagues, and he never spoke to girlfriends when they became ex-girlfriends. But he had managed to pick people up along the way – guys who once worked in record shops[4] that he often went to, guys he played football or squash with, guys from a pub quiz[5] team he once belonged to, that kind of thing – and they sort of did the job. They wouldn't be much use in the unlikely event of some kind of suicidal[6] depression, or the even more unlikely event of a broken heart, but they were
15 pretty good for a game of pool, or a drink and a curry.

No, the evenings were OK; it was the days that tested his patience[7] and creativity, because all of these people were at work – unless they were on paternity leave[8], like John, father of Barney and Imogen, and Will didn't want to see them anyway. His way of dealing with the days was to think of activities as units of time, each unit consisting of about thirty minutes. Whole hours, he found, were
20 more intimidating[9], and most things one could do in a day took half an hour. Reading the paper, having a bath, tidying the flat, watching *Home and Away* and *Countdown*, doing a quick crossword on the toilet, eating breakfast and lunch, going to the local shops ... That was nine units of a twenty unit day (the evenings didn't count) filled by just the basic necessities. In fact, he had reached a stage[10] where he wondered how his friends could juggle[11] life and a job. Life took up so much time,
25 so how could one work *and*, say, take a bath on the same day?

Source: Nick Hornby, 'About a Boy' (abridged and adapted)

1 **lack of** Mangel an │ 2 **disposal** Verfügung │ 3 **resourceful** erfindungsreich │ 4 **record shop** Plattenladen │
5 **pub quiz** Kneipenquiz│ 6 **suicidal** selbstmordgefährdet │ 7 **patience** Geduld │ 8 **paternity leave**
Vaterschaftsurlaub │ 9 **intimidating** einschüchternd │ 10 **stage** hier: Stadium │ 11 **juggle** jonglieren

Comprehension – Analysis – Evaluation

a) *Summarise what we learn about Will's lifestyle and how he feels about it.*

b) *Examine the writer's use of language to describe Will's attitude about time. Give examples from the text.*

c) *Comment on whether you think Will is an example of someone who is living 'the good life'.*

OR

Write a dialogue between Will and one of his friends who has a job, in which they compare their lives.

Green Line 5
Vorschläge zur Leistungsmessung
ISBN: 978-3-12-834254-2

© Ernst Klett Verlag GmbH, Stuttgart 2018 | www.klett.de
Von dieser Druckvorlage ist die Vervielfältigung für den eigenen
Unterrichtsgebrauch gestattet. Die Kopiergebühren sind
abgegolten. Alle Rechte vorbehalten.

Textquellen: Carolyn Jones, Beckenham; *About a Boy* by Nick Hornby, first
published by Victor Gollancz, London, 1998

Comprehension

a) *Read the novel extract and tick ✓ the correct answer(s) to each question.*

1. Will takes pride in the fact that he …

   a) ☐ is a very good swimmer.

   b) ☐ has done lots of good things.

   c) ☐ can deal with having lots of time.

2. Will often spends his evenings with …

   a) ☐ women who were once girlfriends.

   b) ☐ people he knows a little.

   c) ☐ people who aren't important to him.

3. What is Will's attitude about people with kids?

   a) ☐ He wishes he were them.

   b) ☐ He avoids them.

   c) ☐ He understands them.

4. How does Will spend his days?

   a) ☐ He is hardly ever at home.

   b) ☐ He divides his time between home activities and going out.

   c) ☐ He goes out and meets friends.

5. How does Will feel about how other people manage their time?

   a) ☐ insecure

   b) ☐ suspicious

   c) ☐ amazed

6. What is the atmosphere of the text?

   a) ☐ hopeless

   b) ☐ ironic

   c) ☐ funny

b) *Read the text and then the statements. Tick ✓ true or false and give evidence from the text with line numbers.*

	true	false
1. Will thinks that he leads a busy life.		
Evidence:		
2. Will doesn't know any people he can go out with in the evenings.		
Evidence:		
3. Will has nobody he could turn to if he had a serious problem.		
Evidence:		
4. Everyone that Will knows is busy during the day.		
Evidence:		
5. Will has no routine for his daily activities.		
Evidence:		
6. Will has little understanding of how most people live.		
Evidence:		

Green Line 5
Vorschläge zur Leistungsmessung
ISBN: 978-3-12-834254-2

© Ernst Klett Verlag GmbH, Stuttgart 2018 | www.klett.de
Von dieser Druckvorlage ist die Vervielfältigung für den eigenen
Unterrichtsgebrauch gestattet. Die Kopiergebühren sind
abgegolten. Alle Rechte vorbehalten.

Textquellen: Carolyn Jones, Beckenham

4   Reading: How to write a successful CV

Employers receive an average of 60 applicants for every advertisement for a low-skilled job, and 20 for every skilled job. Almost half of these candidates qualify for the role, according to research by the Chartered Institute of Personnel and Development (CIPD). So that makes their CV all the more important when trying to stand out from the crowd[1].

5   Experts say there are some golden rules for getting a CV correct, not least accuracy[2], spelling and grammar. Don't repeat the mistakes, they say, of the applicant who ignored commas when describing his interests as "cooking dogs and interesting people".

The first set of "eyes" to see your CV might be an automated search[3] for key words, so experts suggest applicants make sure mandatory[4] requirements in the job advert are included. Corinne
10   Mills, managing director[5] of Personal Career Management, which provides career coaching, says that digital CVs should be in a simple format and font[6] so readability is not affected[7] on different screens.

Other tips from Mrs Mills, the CIPD, and the National Careers Service include:
- Tailor[8] a CV to a specific job – it is very important to make sure the script is relevant to each
15   job application, rather than sending the same general CV
- Keep it simple – it should be easy to read and use active language. Two pages of A4 is enough with a mini profile included in the first half page
- Include key information – personal details, including name, address, phone number, email address and any professional social media presence[9] should be clear. A date of birth is no
20   longer needed, owing to age discrimination rules. A photo is only required for jobs such as acting and modelling, otherwise it is a matter of choice[10]
- Emphasise achievements – give examples of how targets were exceeded[11] and ideas created, but always be honest
- Check and double check – avoid sloppy[12] errors, take a fresh look the next day and ask for a
25   second opinion from a trusted friend or colleague

Source: www.bbc.com (abridged and adapted)

1 **stand out from the crowd** aus der Menge hervorstechen | 2 **accuracy** Genauigkeit |
3 **automated search** automatische Suche | 4 **mandatory** vorgeschrieben |
5 **managing director** Geschäftsführer/-in | 6 **font** Schriftart | 7 **affect** beeinträchtigen |
8 **tailor** hier: auf etw. zuschneiden | 9 **media presence** Medienpräsenz |
10 **be a matter of choice** im eigenen Ermessen sein | 11 **exceed** übertreffen | 12 **sloppy** schludrig

Comprehension – Analysis – Evaluation

a) *Outline at least five pieces of advice the text gives about writing a successful CV.*

b) *Examine how the writer's use of language makes the factual text above more readable. Give examples from the text.*

c) *Discuss whether you think not requiring the applicant's date of birth and photo on a CV can help prevent discrimination.*

    OR

    Comment on which pieces of advice in the text you think would create the worst impression if you didn't follow them. Give reasons.

Green Line 5
Vorschläge zur Leistungsmessung
ISBN: 978-3-12-834254-2

Textquellen: Carolyn Jones, Beckenham; *How to write a successful CV* by
Kevin Peachey, BBC News, January 12, 2015

Comprehension

a) *Your friend wants to apply for a job and asks you for your help with her CV. Answer her questions according to the information given in the text.*

1. Why is my CV so important? _____

2. How can I show employers that I have studied the job description carefully? _____

   _____

3. I'll impress employers if my CV is the longest, right? _____

4. Do I need to give my date of birth or attach my photo? _____

   _____

5. Can I exaggerate some of my achievements? They'll never know! _____

   _____

b) *Read the job ad and the CV of a student who wants to apply for the job. Make a grid in which you list what's good and bad or unnecessary about the CV according to the advice in the article.*

Summer job for students

Summer is a very busy time for music, sports and other big events. We are looking for students who can help us serve food and drink to the thousands of visitors who will come to enjoy entertainment at some of this city's most exciting locations. You should be sociable, energetic and hard-working. You need experience of serving customers and dealing with money. You should be able to work at different times of day and in different locations. If you like to have fun while you earn some money, please contact us at the address below and attach your CV.

Curriculum Vitae

Personal details:

Name:	Jamie Waldon
Address:	12 Beech Lane, Moseley, Birmingham B4 3LJ
Tel:	04937 8494737
E-mail:	jamwald@smail.co.uk
Date of birth:	19.10.2002

Education: St Thomas Comprehensive scool

Experience: None

Personal profile:

I am looking for a job this summer because I need to earn some money. I don't really mind what I do. I am very sociable – my friends will tell you that I love to have fun! I also think I work hard and have a lot of energy. I am available most mornings and afternoons and am happy to travel to different locations.

c) *Improve the CV so that Jamie could send it to his future employer.*

Green Line 5
Vorschläge zur Leistungsmessung
ISBN: 978-3-12-834254-2

© Ernst Klett Verlag GmbH, Stuttgart 2018 | www.klett.de
Von dieser Druckvorlage ist die Vervielfältigung für den eigenen
Unterrichtsgebrauch gestattet. Die Kopiergebühren sind
abgegolten. Alle Rechte vorbehalten.

Textquellen: Carolyn Jones, Beckenham
Bildquellen: iStockphoto (ProArtWork), Calgary, Alberta

5   Writing: An application letter

Read the advertisement below and write a letter in which you apply for a place on a work experience project.

> You're young, and you're very busy. So why should you spend the little free time you have volunteering? Well, here are a few reasons:
> - You'll do something that makes a meaningful difference – and it feels fantastic!
> - Future employers will be impressed with your work experience!
> - You'll learn new things, meet new people and generally have a great summer!
>
> We are offering positions on four-week work experience projects for people aged 15 to 17 in either July or August this year. With these projects, you'll have the opportunity to gain experience by helping people in your own community. You can choose from the following work experience areas:
> - visiting the elderly and helping them with daily tasks
> - organising activities for local children
> - improving the local environment e.g. planting trees and flowers, cleaning up streets, painting community buildings
> - organising an event to raise money for your community
>
> There are training days on 21st and 22nd June. To apply, please send an application letter to:
>
> Community Summer Work
> Dovedale Road
> Faversham
> Kent ME4 OGE
>
> Make sure you tell us:
> - the month you would like to do your work experience project
> - your main area of interest
> - the skills and experience you could offer us
> - why you are interested in the work experience projects

6   Writing: A job description

a) *Write a job description for the job in one of the pictures.*

flight attendant

children's party organiser

sport shop assistant

b) *Compare two of the jobs and say which you would prefer to have and why.*

Green Line 5
Vorschläge zur Leistungsmessung
ISBN: 978-3-12-834254-2

© Ernst Klett Verlag GmbH, Stuttgart 2018 | www.klett.de
Von dieser Druckvorlage ist die Vervielfältigung für den eigenen
Unterrichtsgebrauch gestattet. Die Kopiergebühren sind
abgegolten. Alle Rechte vorbehalten.

Textquellen: Carolyn Jones, Beckenham
Bildquellen: iStockphoto (RUBEN RAMOS), Calgary, Alberta; shutterstock
(gpointstudio), New York, NY; iStockphoto (EXTREME-PHOTOGRAPHER),
Calgary, Alberta

7 Mediation: Organising a Fair Trade Day

An English friend is organising a Fair Trade Day at her school and has asked you for suggestions. Your German friend organised a Fair Trade Day at her school recently and has written to you about it. She has sent you the e-mail below. Write to your English friend, and tell her about ideas in the e-mail that you think might help her with her school's Fair Trade Day.

Hi! Natürlich kann ich dir ein paar Ideen geben, wie man einen Fair Trade Day organisieren kann! Unser Tag ist wirklich toll geworden! Eigentlich ist das Beste was man tun kann, sich Informationen von der Fair Trade Website zu holen, weil es dort viele Ideen und Ratschläge gibt. Ich erzähle dir einfach mal von unseren beiden erfolgreichsten Aktionen.

Die erste Sache, die wir organisiert haben, war ein Fair Trade Frühstück. Wir haben in der Aula ein paar große Tische und Plakate aufgestellt und die Schüler haben sich ihr Frühstück gekauft, als sie reingekommen sind. Das ganze Geld, das wir damit eingenommen haben, ist an Fair Trade gegangen. Die Idee dahinter war, dass die Schüler nicht nur ein gutes Frühstück haben, sondern sich auch Gedanken darüber machen sollten, woher das Essen und die Getränke eigentlich kommen. Das Motto war „Essen zum Nachdenken!" und wir hatten viele bunte Poster gemacht, die gezeigt haben, woher das Essen kommt. Wir hatten Poster über Orangensaft, Tee, Kakao, Zucker und Bananen und haben damit gezeigt, wie schwer das Leben für die Erzeuger dieser Produkte ist. Wusstest du, dass es weltweit mehr als 500 Millionen Kleinbauern gibt, von denen viele noch nicht einmal genug verdienen, um sich selbst versorgen zu können? Der Klimawandel macht ihnen das Leben sehr schwer und auch große Firmen, die die Bauern dazu drängen, ihre Preise zu senken, damit die Produkte günstig angeboten werden können. Wir hatten allerdings auch ein paar Poster mit guten Nachrichten! Wir haben gezeigt, wie Fair Trade den Menschen in den Produktionsländern hilft, indem sie Bildung und Informationen über neue Produktionstechniken bekommen. Über diese Themen hatten wir uns davor nie richtig Gedanken gemacht, aber an diesem Tag sind wir alle mit dem Gedanken nach Hause gegangen, wie einfach unser Leben hier im Vergleich zu dem in anderen Ländern ist.

Die andere Aktion hatte auch etwas mit Nahrung zu tun, was super ist, weil wir Essen lieben ☺ Wir haben einen Backwettbewerb veranstaltet, der riesigen Spaß gemacht hat und an dem sowohl Lehrer und Eltern als auch Schüler teilnehmen konnten. Es sollten kleine Kuchen gebacken werden und die Regel war, dass nur Fair Trade Produkte verwendet werden durften. Die Jury bestand aus zwei Lehrern, zwei Eltern und zwei Schülern, die alle Kuchen probiert und dann Preise an die Gewinner vergeben haben. Bei einem kleinen Zusatzwettbewerb haben Schüler zwei Kuchen probiert und sollten entscheiden, welcher von beiden nur Fair Trade Produkte enthält. Der Gedanke dahinter war den Schülern zu zeigen, dass Fair Trade Produkte nicht wirklich anders schmecken, sondern nur anders gehandelt werden. Natürlich musste später jeder dabei helfen, alle Kuchen aufzuessen – dieser Teil hat besonders viel Spaß gemacht!

Ich hoffe, dass diese Ideen weiterhelfen. Sag deinem Freund gutes Gelingen von mir!

 Green Line 5
Vorschläge zur Leistungsmessung
ISBN: 978-3-12-834254-2

Textquellen: Carolyn Jones, Beckenham
Bildquellen: shutterstock (vectorfusionart), New York, NY; Alamy stock
photo (MShieldsPhotos), Abingdon, Oxon

8 Vocabulary: A Saturday job → (after Station 1)

Use the correct words to complete the advertisement for a Saturday job. There are four more words than you need.

> hard-working | attach | require | satisfaction | employer | position | people skills | encourage | applicants | passionate | experience | opportunity | reference | responsibility | employees | stand out

The _____ of Visitor Welcome Assistant will _____ you to meet and greet

all visitors to the sports centre, direct them to where they want to go and _____ them

to try different activities. It is a fantastic _____ for young people who want to develop

their _____! The centre is a busy place, so we need people who are both

_____ and _____ about sport. All of our _____ can use our

gym and swimming pool for free when they aren't working, so you could earn money and keep fit!

Just click on the link below to complete the form and send it to us by 31st August. Don't forget to

_____ your CV and give us the name of someone we can ask for a

_____. All _____ will be invited to a training day on 10th September,

when we will select the people we would like to join us. For the right people, this job will bring fun

and useful work _____!

9 Vocabulary: Adjectives → (after Station 1)

Complete the sentences with a suitable adjective.

1. If you want to be successful in life, you have to stay f_____ on your goals.

2. My brother wants to travel the world on his own when he's older,

   but I'm not so a_____!

3. Jack is so m_____! He's always buying the latest gadgets and new clothes.

4. You don't have to speak good French in this job, but it's d_____.

5. My mother is a nurse and says that helping people every day is very f_____.

6. It's not r_____ to expect to succeed in your job if you don't work hard.

7. Jen thinks it's the best thing in the world to be an artist. She's p_____ about her job.

Green Line 5
Vorschläge zur Leistungsmessung
ISBN: 978-3-12-834254-2

© Ernst Klett Verlag GmbH, Stuttgart 2018 | www.klett.de
Von dieser Druckvorlage ist die Vervielfältigung für den eigenen
Unterrichtsgebrauch gestattet. Die Kopiergebühren sind
abgegolten. Alle Rechte vorbehalten.

Textquellen: Carolyn Jones, Beckenham

10 Vocabulary: Using adjectives as nouns → (after Station 2)

*Complete each of these sentences with **the** and an adjective used as a noun.*

1. Life on the streets is very hard for _____, especially in winter.

2. My town has special paths for wheelchair users. It makes life easier for _____.

3. I don't think _____ are always happier than everyone else. Money isn't everything!

4. _____ often stay active these days, even in their eighties and nineties!

5. I want a job that helps _____ because surviving with no money must be very difficult.

6. _____ have their whole lives in front of them, how exciting!

11 Vocabulary: Work activities → (after Station 3)

Look at the pictures and complete the sentences.

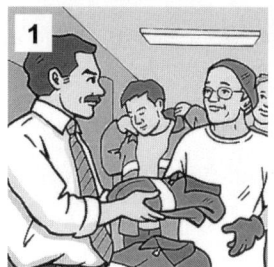   

1. The employer is _____ his employees with uniforms.

2. The boys are _____ cocoa.

3. The girls are _____ boxes.

4. The truck driver is _____ rubbish.

5. The _____ is slicing wood.

6. The factory worker is checking her _____.

7. The volunteers are _____ what they need.

8. The _____ are working together in their office.

12 Language: Improving the style of an application → (after Station 1)

Underline the correct linking adverbs to improve the style of these application sentences.

1. I will finish my exams in late June. **Unfortunately, / Therefore, / However,** I will be able to start work in early July.

2. I have some experience in looking after children. **Moreover, / Therefore, / However,** I have never taught before.

3. I passed my Level 3 swimming exam last month. **Hopefully, / Unfortunately, / However,** my certificate will arrive soon.

4. I do a lot of drama in my free time. **However, / Therefore, / Moreover,** I have good music and dance skills too.

5. I consider myself a good team-player. **Hopefully, / Of course, / Therefore,** I am able to work independently as well.

6. I know the summer camp well. **However, / Therefore, / In fact,** I went there myself when I was ten.

7. I get on very well with all kinds of people. **Of course, / Unfortunately, / However,** this must be an advantage when working with counsellors from all over the world.

8. I am available all of July. **Luckily, / In fact, / Unfortunately,** I have to attend an important family event on the 27th, though.

9. I speak good Spanish. **Therefore, / Luckily, / Hopefully,** my Spanish mother taught me well!

10. We play many different sports at school. **However, / Hopefully, / Therefore,** football is my favourite.

13 Language: A renovating project → (after Station 2)

Describe what Lucy saw/noticed/watched … when she visited a community project.

1. She saw a man _____.

2. _____.

3. _____.

4. _____.

5. _____.

6. _____.

7. _____.

8. _____.

Green Line 5
Vorschläge zur Leistungsmessung
ISBN: 978-3-12-834254-2

Textquellen: Carolyn Jones, Beckenham
Illustratorin: Simone Pahl, Berlin

14 Language: Present participle after verbs of rest and motion → (after Station 2)

Use the pairs of verbs correctly in the sentences from a blog about a charity race Dana took part in last weekend.

> go home / know | catch myself / think | stand / wait | stay / chat | arrive / feel |
> run along / encourage

1. I _____ very nervous.

2. We _____ for half an hour for the race to start.

3. The crowd _____ us.

4. I _____ I was too tired to finish!

5. I _____ to the other runners after the race was over.

6. We _____ we had raised a lot of money for charity!

15 Language: Inversion for emphasis → (after Station 3)

Lily is texting her friend. Invert her sentences for emphasis.

You know that job I applied for? Well, I've just had my interview! (1) I've never felt so nervous! The day started badly. (2) I had hardly got out of bed when my phone rang. It was my Dad – he said he couldn't take me by car so I'd have to go by bus! (3) I only realised then that I was already late! Anyway, I got here just in time and (4) I had no sooner arrived than the organiser came out to greet me. (5) I not only had to answer lots of questions, but I had to give a short presentation too! Then I had to wait for a few minutes afterwards, but soon she came out and told me I'd got the job! (6) I've rarely been so happy!

16 Language: Non-defining relative clauses → (after Station 3)

Use the sentences below to add extra information to the short text about Alex Brodie. In each case, use non-defining relative clauses to combine the sentences.

> Alex Brodie has an important message for all teenagers. He says, "The world needs more young inventors!" His parents have always encouraged him to build and explore things and he reads anything he can find about science. His older brother is very interested in world issues. At the moment he is working on some small building tools. He also posts regular invention videos online.
>
> X ▲ ▼

1. Alex Brodie is a 15-year-old inventor.
2. His parents are both doctors.
3. Science is his favourite subject.
4. His older brother is at university.

5. Alex enjoys discussing world issues with him.
6. His building tools could help people in poorer countries.
7. His videos offer advice to other young inventors.

17   Language: Defining or non-defining clauses? → (after Station 3)

Decide which sentences have defining or non-defining relative clauses. Put in commas where you need them but be careful not to put them where you don't need them!

Last Friday, my class had a work experience day that was really interesting. I was in the group who wanted to work with animals and we were sent to the office of an organisation which collects food, beds and toys for homeless dogs. First, the students who had all arrived ready for a busy day packed boxes. Then, we loaded them onto the organisation truck which was waiting outside and drove off to deliver them. It was a day which taught us a lot about teamwork. The people who worked at the shelters were very friendly – and we met some wonderful dogs who we wanted to take home with us!

18   Language: Do/does/did for emphasis → (after Station 3)

Read the dialogue between two colleagues. Then complete Robbie's lines to emphasise his reaction to Ivy's questions/statements.

Ivy: You didn't like that book I lent you about life in the future, did you?

Robbie: Actually, I _____ and I read it to the end! Now I bet that _____ surprise you!

Ivy: Ha, but you _____ say you don't enjoy science fiction films much, right?

Robbie: Wrong again! I _____ like them! I can see that _____ come as a surprise for you!

Ivy: Hmm. Maybe I'm thinking of your brother. He doesn't read or watch films much, does he?

Robbie: Well, he doesn't read, but he _____ watch lots of films. He's more interested in the past than the future, although last week I _____ see him watching a film about life in 100 years.

Klett   **Green Line 5**   Vorschläge zur Leistungsmessung   ISBN: 978-3-12-834254-2
Textquellen: Carolyn Jones, Beckenham

Text smart 2 Informative texts

1   Social media is harming the mental health of teenagers. The state has to act

June Eric Oderie | Wednesday 16 September 2015

The digital landscape has put increased[1] pressure[2] on teenagers today, and we feel it. There are so many social media channels: Facebook, Twitter, Instagram, Snapchat, Tumblr, you name it. I made a decision to avoid Snapchat and Instagram because of the social pressure I saw them putting on my 14-year-old little sister. If my mum turned off the WiFi at 11pm, my sister would beg[3] me to turn my phone into a hotspot. She always needed to load her Snapchat stories one more time, or to reply to a message that had come in two minutes ago because she didn't want her friend to feel ignored. If I said no, saying she could reply in the morning, I'd get the "You're ruining my social life" speech. Even as a teenager as well, I can't really understand why people do this.

A new study has found that teenagers who use social media during the night could be affecting their sleep and increasing[4] their risk of angst and depression. Teenagers spoke about the pressure they felt to make themselves available 24/7, and the resulting angst if they did not reply immediately to texts or posts. Teens are so emotional about social media that a fifth of secondary school pupils will wake up at night and log on, just to make sure they don't miss out.

It's becoming more and more obvious how the pressures of social media affect teenage girls much more than boys. I can see it all around me. Pressure to be perfect. To look perfect, act perfect, have the perfect body, the perfect friends, the perfect amount of likes on Instagram. Perfect, perfect, perfect. And if you don't meet these high standards, then the self-hating and bullying begins.

What is really worrying is that time and time again, these studies demonstrate that the health of teenagers, especially teenage girls, is at risk. We know this. We know that these studies demonstrate that we have to introduce personal, social and health education in every school and make sure it covers issues from healthy eating to sleeping. And yet, the government will not act. So I ask: what are we waiting for? What has to happen before we do something?

Source: www.theguardian.com (abridged and adapted)

1 **increased** erhöht | 2 **pressure** Druck | 3 **beg** (an)betteln | 4 **increase** erhöhen

*Read the article above and the two texts **A** and **B** below. Explain which text below is an analysis or a summary. Do you think the summary and the analysis are successful? Explain why/why not and tell what is wrong/missing.*

| **A** In her online article published in the Guardian, June Eric Oderie argued that the state has to protect teenagers, especially girls, from the pressures of social media.
The author illustrated the problem by giving the example of her younger sister, who felt that she had to be online in order to keep up her social life.
According to the author, studies showed that teenagers' use of social media at night was "increasing their risk of angst and depression."
The author concludes with an appeal to the government to help by making personal, social and health education part of the curriculum at all schools. | **B** The writer outlines the negative effects of being online 24/7. She chooses her sister as an example and describes how she feels when she is not online 24/7. I am sure that this story makes the article more interesting for teenage readers as they can identify with the sister.
The author backs up her arguments by referring to studies which have examined the negative effects of social media on teenagers' health.
The aim of the article is to ask the government to help by making personal, social and health education part of the curriculum at all schools.
The author concludes with an appeal to the readers by asking, "What has to happen before we do something?" |

2   A summary: Teenagers' IQ scores can rise or fall sharply during adolescence

Ed Yong | Wednesday 19 October 2011

A study suggests IQ is not stable during teenage years as was thought but changes as the brain develops. IQ scores can change dramatically in teenage years in parallel with changes to the brain, according to a study that suggests being careful in using the 11+ exam for grammar school entrance to predict potential.

IQ is thought to be stable across a person's life. Childhood scores are often used to predict the results of future education and job possibilities as an adult. But the study suggests scores are surprisingly variable[1].

Robert Sternberg from Oklahoma State University, who studies intelligence but was not in the research team, said: "A testing industry has developed around the idea that IQ is relatively fixed in the early years of life. This study shows in a convincing way that meaningful changes can happen throughout the teenage years."

Our intelligence is not fixed, he said: "People who are mentally[2] active will likely benefit, and the couch potatoes who do not exercise themselves intellectually will pay a price."

Sue Ramsden from University College London chose 33 pupils aged 12 to 16, from high achievers at 11+ to struggling students. She tested their IQ in 2004, and again three to four years later, and also analysed their brains. The average[3] of all scores stayed the same across the years, but individual IQ scores rose or fell by as many as 21 points, a large difference – enough to take a person of "average" intelligence to "gifted[4]" status, or back again. The teens divided between those whose IQ improved and those whose IQ worsened. "It was not the case that young low achievers got better, and the young high achievers averaged out. Some highs got even better, and some lows got even worse," said Price.

The study challenges a long-standing view of intelligence as fixed. Alfred Binet, father of modern intelligence tests, believed mental development ended at 16, while child psychologist Jean Piaget thought it ended even earlier.

The team now wants to know what causes this change in IQ: brain development, or educational factors that stimulate some skills but not others; and also if changes are teenage only or whether IQ can change as dramatically in adults. Until then the message for children, parents and teachers is, as Ramsden writes in *Nature*: "This study gives hope to some whose intelligence may improve, and a warning that early achievers may not reach their potential."

Source: www.theguardian.com (abridged and adapted)

1 **variable** veränderlich | 2 **mental** geistig | 3 **average** Durchschnitt, durchschnittlich | 4 **gifted** hochbegabt

Highlight important key words in the text and write down important details in the margin. Then write a summary of the article in about 130 words.

3   An analysis

Imagine that you work for Issues4Teens, an online magazine for young people. This month's topic is "IQ". You are asked if you think this article should be published in the magazine. In order to judge this, analyse the following points:

- *if the structure is clear,*
- *how well its message is communicated,*
- *how interesting the text is for a teenage reader.*

Now write a full analysis. Remember to use appropriate language and explain your opinion with supporting examples from the text. Then give your opinion on whether to publish the article.

Green Line 5
Vorschläge zur Leistungsmessung
ISBN: 978-3-12-834254-2

© Ernst Klett Verlag GmbH, Stuttgart 2018 | www.klett.de
Von dieser Druckvorlage ist die Vervielfältigung für den eigenen
Unterrichtsgebrauch gestattet. Die Kopiergebühren sind
abgegolten. Alle Rechte vorbehalten.

Textquellen: Pauline Ashworth, Stuttgart; *Teenagers' IQ scores can rise or fall sharply during adolescence* by Ed Yong, The Guardian, October 19, 2011

Unit 3 California dreaming

⊙ **1 Listening: Historical events in Hollywood films**

Listen to the dialogue between students and their History teacher. Complete the sentences in 8 words or less.

1. Today the students are discussing films that are _____.

2. In Hollywood films, historical events are sometimes adapted in order to _____

_____.

3. The film '42' tells about the life of Jackie Robinson, who was a _____

_____.

4. Although the film makes it sound this way, he was not the only _____

_____.

5. The film 'Pocahontas' presents Pocahontas as _____

who has romantic feelings for an _____ named John Smith.

6. In fact, she was still _____ at the time she met him.

7. Some people get their knowledge about _____.

8. The way Hollywood films show history can have an important effect on how we think about

_____. (1 thing)

9. One student thinks that films can influence _____.

10. The last student has the opinion that films should mainly _____.

Green Line 5
Vorschläge zur Leistungsmessung
ISBN: 978-3-12-834254-2

Textquellen: Katie Hoffman, Olathe, Kansas
Bildquellen: shutterstock (hans engbers), New York, NY; Moviestore
collection Ltd / Alamy Stock Foto, London. POCAHONTAS (ANI - 1995)
ANIMATED CREDIT DISNEY.

2   Listening: Harvey Milk

Listen to the radio show. Choose the correct answers. There can be more than one correct answer.

1. The radio DJ is talking about …

   a) ☐ an event that happened to a listener.

   b) ☐ an event that happened 30 years ago.

   c) ☐ an event that happened the same day as the show but in a different year.

2. Harvey Milk …

   a) ☐ was very open about being gay.

   b) ☐ only talked to his closest friends about being gay.

   c) ☐ only talked to the gay community.

3. In the 1970s, Harvey Milk …

   a) ☐ became a government official.

   b) ☐ moved to Los Angeles.

   c) ☐ fought for gay rights.

4. In the 1970s, …

   a) ☐ the gay community experienced a lot of illness.

   b) ☐ the gay community was getting quieter.

   c) ☐ the gay community was getting larger.

5. Harvey supported policy changes which helped …

   a) ☐ gay communities.

   b) ☐ women with children who had to work.

   c) ☐ big companies and businesses.

6. Dan White …

   a) ☐ was a government official.

   b) ☐ supported Harvey's policy changes.

   c) ☐ shot Harvey Milk.

7. After Harvey was killed, more than 25,000 people …

   a) ☐ became violent and destroyed government offices.

   b) ☐ walked peacefully through the streets to remember him.

   c) ☐ celebrated his life by having a concert.

8. In the film 'Milk', …

   a) ☐ all of the details are correct.

   b) ☐ some of the details aren't totally correct.

   c) ☐ Harvey was killed because he was gay and supported gay rights.

Green Line 5
Vorschläge zur Leistungsmessung
ISBN: 978-3-12-834254-2

Textquellen: Katie Hoffman, Olathe, Kansas
Bildquellen: Alamy stock photo (Robert Clay), Abingdon, Oxon; Alamy stock
photo (Robert Clay), Abingdon, Oxon

B

A

A/B A/B

A *This picture is part of a news report. What does it show and what do you think the story behind the picture is?*

B *This picture is part of a news report. What does it show and what do you think the story behind the picture is?*

Partner A/B (Set 1): *A teenager in northern Australia jumped into a river that is known for its dangerous crocodiles. He was dared by his friends to jump. (= Er wurde von Freunden herausgefordert, als Mutprobe zu springen.) The teenager was attacked by a crocodile and received serious injuries to his arm.*
Discuss the behaviour of the teenager and his friends and try to come to an agreement about the following points:
- *Who is most responsible for the injuries – the teeenager or his friends?*
- *Should the friends be punished for daring him to jump?*
- *What kind of punishment would be appropriate?*

Partner A/B (Set 2): *You and your partner want to interview the person with the crocodile or the spider as part of a news report for teenage listeners. Which one will both of you choose and why? Agree on questions that you want to ask that person.*

A   *Look at the film still below.*
a) *Describe the still. Say where the scene is set and analyse the film techniques used.*
b) *Explain why this scene is important for the clip.*

B   *Look at the film still below.*
a) *Describe the still. Say where the scene is set and analyse the film techniques used.*
b) *Explain why this scene is important for the clip.*

Partner A/B (Set 1): *Discuss why this short film is an example for the genre crime. Give specific examples and reasons why they are effective.*

Partner A/B (Set 2): *The screenwriter has three different ideas (A–C) for the next part of the clip. Discuss with your partner which idea you think would be best. Give reasons for your opinion.*

3 Optionen wie der Film weitergehen könnte

A   Greg runs away from the police and hides somewhere in London. He hopes they don't find him.

B   Greg runs away from the police because he has an idea where to find Maya. But he can't find her.

C   Greg runs away from the police because he has an idea where to find Maya. He finds her.

Discuss with your partner how you would film the idea you have chosen above. Think about the setting(s), body language and facial expressions, shots and audiovisual effects. Give reasons for your choices.

B A

A/B A/B

B

A

A/B A/B

A *Look at the picture and imagine that you are one of the teenagers who is waiting for an interview for a part-time job. Say who you are and give information about yourself. Say how you are feeling and what questions you might ask during the interview.*

B *Look at the picture and imagine that you are one of the teenagers who is waiting for an interview for a part-time job. Say who you are and give information about yourself. Say how you are feeling and what questions you might ask during the interview.*

Partner A/B (Set 1): *You and your partner are planning to interview applicants for a job at the local community centre. Discuss what skills you want your applicants to have and what questions you are going to ask them in order to choose the right person for the job.*

Partner A/B (Set 2): *One of you is the shop assistant at a sports shop. The other is a customer who wants to know why the prices are quite high compared to prices in other shops. Act out the conversation.*

 **A** *In your own words, say what you think the quotes are about.*
Explain the difference between fame and success.
What do you think brings (more) happiness to a famous person who already has lots of money and power?

> "Don't confuse fame with success."

Erma Louise Bombeck, American writer

> "My happiness doesn't come from money or fame. My happiness comes from seeing life without struggle."

Nicki Minaj, singer and songwriter

 **B** *In your own words, say what you think the quotes are about.*
Which would you choose: being famous even though you don't really like what you do or loving what you do even though it won't make you famous?

> "I think the worst thing that can happen to a good actor is fame."

Vera Farmiga, American actress

> "When I started acting almost 50 years ago, it wasn't about fame. It was about acting."

Maggie Smith, British actress

Partner A/B (Set 1): *You and your partner founded a start-up company and became rich and famous very quickly. Discuss and then agree on how you are going to spend a million dollars to become happier – and perhaps even more famous.*

Partner A/B (Set 2): *A new museum is about to open in Germany. The museum is going to have a small section with no more than eight wax figures in it. Discuss who you think should be standing in it. Give reasons for your opinions.*

B

A

A/B A/B

3 Reading: The Circuit[1]

'The Circuit' by Francisco Jiménez is a novel based on the author's journey from Mexico to the United States as a child. Francisco and his family travel from Mexico to California so they can have a better life. Every year they move from one place to the next between the same
5 *few cities and work on the farms there, picking fruits and vegetables. Because they move every season, it is difficult to make friends.*
In this extract, Francisco asks his older brother, Roberto, about his first experience at an American school.

"I remember being hit on the wrists with a twelve-inch[2] ruler because I did not follow directions in
10 class," Roberto answered in a mildly[3] angry tone when I asked him about his first year of school. "But how could I?" he continued, "the teacher gave them in English."
"So what did you do?" I asked, rubbing[4] my wrists.

"I always guessed what the teacher wanted me to do. And when she did not use the ruler on me, I knew I had guessed right," he responded. "Some of the kids made fun of me when I tried to say
15 something in English and got it wrong," he went on. "I had to repeat first grade."

I wish I had not asked him, but he was the only one in the family, including Papá and Mamá, who had attended[5] school. I walked away. I did not speak or understand English either, and I already felt anxious[6]. Besides[7], I was excited about going to school for the first time that following Monday. It was late January and we had just returned, a week before, from Corcoran where my family picked
20 cotton[8]. We settled in "Tent City," a labor camp[9] owned by Sheehey Strawberry Farms located about ten miles east of Santa Maria.

On our first day of school, Roberto and I got up early. I dressed in a pair of overalls[10], which I hated because they had suspenders[11], and a flannel checkered shirt[12], which Mamá had bought at the Goodwill store. As I put on my cap, Roberto reminded me that it was bad manners to wear a hat
25 indoors. I thought of leaving it at home so that I would not make the mistake of forgetting to take it off in class, but I decided to wear it. Papá always wore a cap and I did not feel completely dressed for school without it.

Source: Francisco Jiménez, 'The Circuit' (abridged and adapted)

1 **circuit** Kreislauf │ 2 **inch** *Längeneinheit (2,5 cm)* │ 3 **mildly** etwas │ 4 **rub** reiben │ 5 **attend** besuchen │
6 **anxious** ängstlich; unruhig │ 7 **besides** außerdem │ 8 **cotton** Baumwolle │ 9 **labor camp** Arbeitslager │
10 **overalls** Latzhose │ 11 **suspenders** Hosenträger │ 12 **flannel checkered shirt** kariertes Flanellhemd

Comprehension – Analysis – Evaluation

a) *Describe Francisco's experience of preparing to go to an American school.*

b) *Give a character description of Francisco. Based on his impressions and how he tells the story, what can you say about him?*

c) *Invent the next part of the story. What happens during Francisco's first day of school? How does he feel about going to an American school?*

OR

Imagine that you are one of the kids in Francisco's class. Write a diary entry about meeting him. What do you notice about him? How do you think he feels? What might he expect? What might he fear?

Green Line 5
Vorschläge zur Leistungsmessung
ISBN: 978-3-12-834254-2

Textquellen: Katie Hoffman, Olathe, Kansas; *The Circuit* by Francisco
Jiménez, first published by University of New Mexico Press, Albuquerque,
1997
Bildquellen: Alamy Stock Photo (ML Harris), Abingdon, Oxon

Comprehension

a) *Read the text and then the statements. Tick ✓ true or false and give evidence from the text with line numbers where you found the answers.*

	true	false
1. Roberto liked his first year of school in California.		
Evidence:		
2. It was easy for Roberto to understand what his teacher said.		
Evidence:		
3. The other kids helped Roberto learn English.		
Evidence:		
4. Roberto was not very successful in school the first year.		
Evidence:		
5. Francisco is looking forward to going to school.		
Evidence:		

b) *Read the text again and complete the sentences using your own words.*

1. Roberto's teacher didn't show any understanding for _____.

2. Roberto was the first person in his family to _____.

3. Francisco wishes he hadn't asked Roberto about school because _____

_____.

4. Francisco is afraid that school will be difficult for him because _____

_____.

5. Francisco and his family live in _____.

6. Francisco decides to _____ even though _____

_____ because _____.

7. The title of the story, 'The Circuit', was probably chosen because it symbolizes different aspects

of the life Francisco and his family lead, such as _____

_____.

Green Line 5
Vorschläge zur Leistungsmessung
ISBN: 978-3-12-834254-2

© Ernst Klett Verlag GmbH, Stuttgart 2018 | www.klett.de
Von dieser Druckvorlage ist die Vervielfältigung für den eigenen
Unterrichtsgebrauch gestattet. Die Kopiergebühren sind
abgegolten. Alle Rechte vorbehalten.

Textquellen: Katie Hoffman, Olathe, Kansas

4 Reading: California's Latest Trend: Forest Bathing

In modern American society, time spent relaxing outdoors is not an important part of most people's days. In fact, 87% of our days are spent indoors, working long hours, performing household chores, watching television or sitting at the computer. Even our children spend on average between five and seven hours a day in a classroom, with an additional 30 minutes to one hour each afternoon and/or

5 night doing homework. Kids are more likely than their parents to participate in outdoor activities organized by their schools or communities, but an increasing amount of their free time is spent on social media or playing video games. And let's not forget that living in the US requires a car – 6% of our time each day is spent driving to our destination. It's no surprise, then, that Americans are stressed out. In fact, stress is making us sick. Researchers estimate that diseases linked to stress

10 at work or at home cost $125 to $190 billion a year.

California's latest trend in health and fitness may be the solution. It's a practice called 'forest bathing' and it comes from Japan. In Japan, where cultural expectations are high, forest bathing has become a part of the medical system. Research has shown that spending time in nature reduces stress, tension[1] and anxiety[2]. People report less negative thinking and less overthinking[3]. Memory

15 has also been shown to improve.

Forest bathing is not yet included in California's medical system, but forest bathing groups have been set up throughout the state, with guides who take groups of people to green areas in and outside the city. But how, you might be wondering, is it any different from hiking, riding a bike or having a picnic outdoors? With forest bathing, there is no destination. A guided session is one mile

20 or less, but lasts two to four hours. The idea is to take a break, slow down, and experience your environment through your senses. You have to be willing to leave that cell phone at home!
As we all know, when California catches a cold, the rest of the country sneezes[4]. So watch for forest bathing groups to arrive in your area soon!

1 **tension** Anspannung | 2 **anxiety** Beunruhigung; Angst | 3 **overthinking** Grübeln | 4 **sneeze** niesen

Comprehension – Analysis – Evaluation

a) *Outline the information in the text about the new trend of 'forest bathing' in California.*

b) *Examine the author's view about forest bathing. Give examples from the text of what the author says and how he says it that show his view.*

c) *Write an article for your school's online newspaper in which you briefly describe the concept of forest bathing and then discuss whether it should be introduced as an activity at your school.*

OR

Compare what you know about 'forest bathing' from the text to other ways of relaxing and spending time outdoors.

Green Line 5
Vorschläge zur Leistungsmessung
ISBN: 978-3-12-834254-2

© Ernst Klett Verlag GmbH, Stuttgart 2018 | www.klett.de
Von dieser Druckvorlage ist die Vervielfältigung für den eigenen
Unterrichtsgebrauch gestattet. Die Kopiergebühren sind
abgegolten. Alle Rechte vorbehalten.

Textquellen: Katie Hoffman, Olathe, Kansas
Bildquellen: 123rf (racorn), Nidderau; 123rf (mavoimage), Nidderau

Comprehension

a) *Answer these questions in 10 words or less. You do not need to write complete sentences.*

1. Why are Americans stressed out? _____

2. Name two things that American children do in their free time. _____

_____

3. What is forest bathing? _____

4. What are three benefits of forest bathing? _____

_____

5. Why is it important to leave your cell phone at home? _____

_____

6. Explain the expression "When California catches a cold, the rest of the country sneezes".

_____

7. What are two characteristics which describe the writing style of this text? _____

_____

b) *Use their context to explain what these words mean in your own words. Write your own short definition for each of them.*

1. trend (headline; line 11) _____

2. increasing (line 6) _____

3. expectation (line 12) _____

4. to last (line 20) _____

5. to slow down (line 20) _____

6. to be willing (line 21) _____

Green Line 5
Vorschläge zur Leistungsmessung
ISBN: 978-3-12-834254-2
Textquellen: Katie Hoffman, Olathe, Kansas

5 Writing: A handout

You must give a presentation to your class on the topic of the water shortage in the world, with California as an example. Read the text and look at the cartoon. Use the skills and tips you learned in Unit 3 and create the text for a handout. Add additional relevant information from the Unit to make the handout more interesting.

Because of better medical services and living longer lives, the total number of people on earth doubled in less than 50 years after 1950. The world population is now more than 7.5 billion people, and it is expected to increase to 9 billion by 2044. This means that the use of water for drinking, cleaning, food production and preparation and many other human activities has also significantly increased. Although water covers more than 70% of the earth's surface, less than 3% of water on earth is fresh water which is currently available for human use.

Scientists say there is a global water crisis which affects all continents and billions of people, both physically and emotionally. When there is less clean water to drink, there is more disease. When there is a water shortage, food production is less successful, there are fewer jobs and people have more difficulties buying food for their families. Such living conditions increase people's stress and affect the opportunities people have for education, training and healthy, happy lifestyles. These and other effects of water shortage show why the global water crisis has become one of the top three global problems today.

6 Writing: Interpreting diagrams

Look at the two graphs below, then do the exercises.

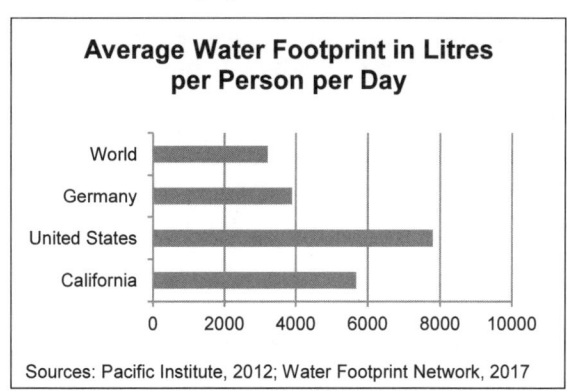

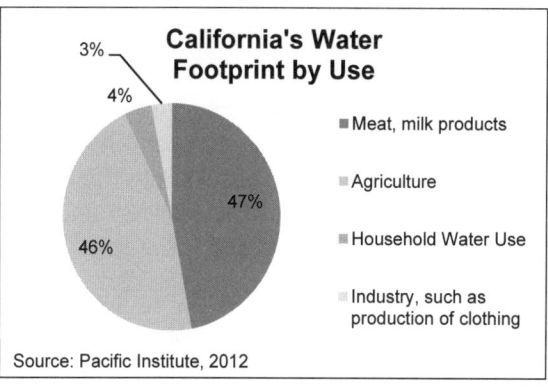

a) *Explain what the two graphs tell you about water use in California.*

b) *Based on the information you see here, comment on changes people in California could make to save the most water and prevent a water shortage in the future.*

Green Line 5
Vorschläge zur Leistungsmessung
ISBN: 978-3-12-834254-2

© Ernst Klett Verlag GmbH, Stuttgart 2018 | www.klett.de
Von dieser Druckvorlage ist die Vervielfältigung für den eigenen
Unterrichtsgebrauch gestattet. Die Kopiergebühren sind
abgegolten. Alle Rechte vorbehalten.

Textquellen: Katie Hoffman, Olathe, Kansas
Bildquellen: www.CartoonStock.com (Fischer, Ed), Bath

41

7 Mediation: Hollywood, here I come?

You get an e-mail from your friend Brian whose family has just moved to California due to his parents working in San Francisco now. He tells you how much he enjoys being so close to Hollywood and that he is thinking about dropping out of school – he wants to run away to L.A. and become an actor. He has already collected some adverts of drama schools in L.A. and is applying now. You have found the following article. Tell Brian what it tells you about such drama schools, the pros and cons of this profession and give him advice.

Der lange Weg zur Filmkarriere

Ein Star vor der Kamera zu werden, ist für viele ein Traum. Von der Hoffnung auf eine rasante Karriere profitieren auch unzählige Workshops, Akademien, Kurse. Aber Crashkurse führen nur selten ans Ziel. Wer als Schauspieler auf Dauer überleben will, muss den harten Weg über Schauspielschulen gehen.
Für den Sprung ins Film- und Fernsehgeschäft braucht man einen langen Atem, warnen Experten.

In der Regel führt an einer klassischen Schauspielausbildung über mehrere Jahre kein Weg vorbei. Blitz-Ausbildungen sieht man bei der Zentralen Bühnen-, Fernseh- und Filmvermittlung (ZBF) der Bundesagentur für Arbeit in Bonn äußerst skeptisch: „Egal ob auf der Bühne oder vor der Kamera: Ohne eine fundierte Schauspielausbildung geht es kaum."

Während Anbieter von Crashkursen mit unrealistischen Karriereversprechen locken, empfiehlt Kerwer eine drei- bis vierjährige Ausbildung, wie sie in Deutschland die staatlichen Schauspielschulen sowie einige renommierte Privatschulen anbieten. Karriere ohne mehrjährige Schulung – das ist nach Kerwers Einschätzung höchstens in TV-Seifenopern möglich: "Und ich habe Zweifel, ob man damit langfristig seinen Lebensunterhalt verdienen kann."

Der Berufsverband Deutscher Schauspieler beklagt ein mangelndes Niveau vieler Kurse für Filmschauspieler. Vorsicht sei besonders bei diffusen Ausbildungen wie „Show-Training" geboten. Für miserablen Unterricht forderten Anbieter solcher Seminare hohe Gebühren.

Hat man schon eine Bühnenausbildung hinter sich, ergeben filmspezifische Crashkurse nach Einschätzung der ZBF und des Schauspielerverbandes durchaus Sinn. Dabei könnten Schauspieler lernen, sich vor der Kamera richtig zu verhalten oder sich auf ein Casting vorzubereiten. Vor einer Kursbuchung sollten die Anbieter aber genau geprüft werden. Verspricht ein Veranstalter eine rasante Karriere, rät er: „Hände weg!"

Auf der Überholspur nach Hollywood? Mit solchen Versprechen will etwa die Schauspielakademie „Mallorca Film Academy" nichts zu tun haben. Die Schule, in deren Beirat auch die Regisseure Dieter Wedel und Detlev Buck sitzen, verspricht ihren Kunden lediglich eine fundierte Ausbildung in Teilbereichen wie etwa dem „Camera Acting", dem Schauspiel vor der Kamera.

Wer das Einmaleins des Schauspiels beherrscht und sich auch mit der Kamera vertraut gemacht hat, ist für die Film- und Fernsehbranche gerüstet. Doch bis zum Star ist es trotzdem ein steiniger Weg: In Zeiten sinkender Werbeeinnahmen bevorzugen die TV-Programmstrategen billige Formate wie Talk- oder Gerichtsshows gegenüber teuren Filmproduktionen. Zudem werden Produktionskosten gedrosselt und Drehzeiten verkürzt. „Es ist ein knochenharter Job, und vor Arbeitslosigkeit ist niemand gefeit", sagt Wolfgang Klein.

Source: www.spiegel.de (abridged)

Green Line 5
Vorschläge zur Leistungsmessung
ISBN: 978-3-12-834254-2

© Ernst Klett Verlag GmbH, Stuttgart 2018 | www.klett.de
Von dieser Druckvorlage ist die Vervielfältigung für den eigenen
Unterrichtsgebrauch gestattet. Die Kopiergebühren sind
abgegolten. Alle Rechte vorbehalten.

Textquellen: Katie Hoffman, Olathe, Kansas; *Der lange Weg zur Filmkarriere*
by Julia Deppe, Spiegel Online, June 18, 2004
Bildquellen: iStockphoto (rodolfo_salgado), Calgary, Alberta

8 Vocabulary: Character traits → (after Station 1)

Match the character traits with their definition.

1. realistic   _____   a) friendly and social

2. optimistic   _____   b) practical or sensible about what can happen or what can be expected

3. relaxed   _____   c) able to accept when there are problems; tolerant

4. outgoing   _____   d) having strong feelings about something

5. persistent   _____   e) hopeful about the future

6. patient   _____   f) calm; not feeling stressed

7. confident   _____   g) positive and certain about one's skills and abilities

8. passionate   _____   h) continuing with an opinion or action even when there are difficulties

9 Vocabulary: Collocations → (after Station 2)

Put the words or phrases together to make collocations. Then use them in the correct sentences.

entertainment | start-up | try | chalk | sports | shoot | keep | strong	+	a film | company | craze | economy| it up to experience | industry| your luck| their head above water

1. Did you know that Hollywood directors will pay you between $1,000 and $5,000 per day to

    _____ at your home?

2. Be careful ... the latest _____ isn't always the best way to help you get

    fit. It might even be dangerous for your health!

3. In a _____, people feel more confident and take more risks with their

    careers and businesses.

4. A _____ works to find innovative solutions to a problem. Sometimes

    they struggle to _____ and 90% of them end up failing.

5. If you decide to _____ in the _____, you'll need

    to make smart choices to increase your chances of success. For example, be active on social

    media and use every opportunity to build your network. And if one job doesn't work out, just

    _____ and move on to the next thing!

Green Line 5
Vorschläge zur Leistungsmessung
ISBN: 978-3-12-834254-2

Textquellen: Katie Hoffman, Olathe, Kansas

10   Vocabulary: Natural disasters → (after Station 3)

Complete the text with the correct words from Station 3.

A natural disaster is any big event in nature that causes a lot of _____ to people, homes, and

businesses in the area. Examples include _____, which can be caused by drought or human

behavior, and _____, which are caused by heavy rain or big storms. _____

there were 380 natural disasters per year between 2005 and 2014. There was only a _____

increase in natural disasters from 330 in 2014 to 376 in 2015. One of the worst natural disasters in

_____ was the earthquake in Haiti in 2010, which killed more than 200,000 people.

At least 3 million people required _____ services, but it was very difficult to _____

those services because so much was destroyed. Many scientists believe _____ is

linked to these weather events, and they can _____ to increase in the future.

11   Language: Working at an internet start-up → (after Station 1)

Complete the dialogue with the correct form of the simple present or present progressive.

Mark: Hey Sara, _____ (catch) the bus early tomorrow morning?

Sara: Yes, I think it _____ (leave) at 6:45 on Mondays. Is that the one you

_____ (take)?

Mark: That's the plan. _____ (eat) before you go or when you get there?

Sara: I _____ (eat) breakfast at home.

Mark: Why? The cafés there are awesome!

Sara: I know, but I won't have much time to eat.

Mark: Well, I _____ (meet) my team for breakfast and brainstorming at 8.

We _____ (discuss) new ideas for Earth Day.

Sara: My boss isn't quite so relaxed. Our meeting _____ (start) at 7:30.

It _____ (end) at 10, then my busy Monday really _____ (get started).

I _____ (not go) to the gym tomorrow because we _____ (work) late.

Klett

Green Line 5
Vorschläge zur Leistungsmessung
ISBN: 978-3-12-834254-2

© Ernst Klett Verlag GmbH, Stuttgart 2018 | www.klett.de
Von dieser Druckvorlage ist die Vervielfältigung für den eigenen
Unterrichtsgebrauch gestattet. Die Kopiergebühren sind
abgegolten. Alle Rechte vorbehalten.

Textquellen: Katie Hoffman, Olathe, Kansas

12   Language: Off to Hollywood → (after Station 1)

Before Alex left for Hollywood, a friend tried to prepare him for the difficulties of becoming an actor. Use the future progressive to make his friend's statements. Write the sentences on an extra sheet of paper.

1. You / probably / not live / your dream / right away.
2. You / go / to one audition after another / at the beginning.
3. You / wait / in line for hours / with other people / who also dream of becoming actors.
4. I'm sure / your parents / ask / if / you / come home soon.
5. You / entertain / people / on the street / to make money.
6. Film directors / look for / 'extras' / for their movies. That could be your lucky chance!

13   Language: One possible world → (after Station 1)

Look at the pictures. What will or will not have been done in this world by the year 2050? A futurist (someone who makes predictions about the future) tells us what he thinks. Complete the sentences and describe the pictures by using the future perfect.

1. By 2050, car companies _____. (produce)

2. By 2035, we _____. (clean up)

3. Hopefully, in 25 years countries _____. (end)

4. But humans _____. (not find)

5. And most of them still _____. (not stop)

6. But scientists _____ to make people live longer. (develop)

Green Line 5
Vorschläge zur Leistungsmessung
ISBN: 978-3-12-834254-2

© Ernst Klett Verlag GmbH, Stuttgart 2018 | www.klett.de
Von dieser Druckvorlage ist die Vervielfältigung für den eigenen
Unterrichtsgebrauch gestattet. Die Kopiergebühren sind
abgegolten. Alle Rechte vorbehalten.

Textquellen: Katie Hoffman, Olathe, Kansas
Illustratorin: Simone Pahl, Berlin

14 Language: Sequoia National Park → (after Station 2)

*Decide if you need **the**, **a/an** or no article (—). Circle the correct answer.*

Sequoia National Park is **a / an / the** national park located in **a / the / —** southern California's Sierra

Nevada mountains. It is one of **a / the / —** most popular national parks in the United States.

Sequoia National Park has many beautiful things to see, but it is particularly famous for **a / the / —**

giant sequoia trees which form **a / an / the** giant forest. Also called 'The Land of the Giants', this

forest is **an / the / —** home to more than 8,000 sequoias, which are some of **a / the / —** largest and

oldest trees on earth. Some sequoias grow as tall as **a / an / the** average 26-floor building and as

wide as **a / an / the** city street. **A / An / —** giant sequoia tree can live for more than 3,000 years.

Some visitors have described the experience of visiting **a / the / —** Sequoia National Park like

walking through **a / an / —** magical cathedral.

15 Language: Article or no article? → (after Station 2)

*Read each pair of sentences. Choose the correct abstract noun below and use it in both sentences.
One sentence requires a definite article and one does not.*

| ability | competition | culture | education | risk |

1. The government of California is responsible for _____ of more than 6 million

   children in more than 10,000 schools. / The future of _____ depends on how much

   money they are willing to spend on it.

2. _____ is what makes companies in Silicon Valley so successful. / The worldwide

   economy has increased _____ among countries to attract talented workers.

3. Some people say without _____, there is no growth. / People who move to

   California to become actors know _____ is high that they will not succeed.

4. _____ to learn quickly is one of the characteristics that companies look for in their

   employees. / If you also have _____ to communicate well with others, you will find

   a job more easily.

5. What is the role of music in _____ of a city or country? / Music communicates ideas

   about _____ and identity.

Green Line 5
Vorschläge zur Leistungsmessung
ISBN: 978-3-12-834254-2

© Ernst Klett Verlag GmbH, Stuttgart 2018 | www.klett.de
Von dieser Druckvorlage ist die Vervielfältigung für den eigenen
Unterrichtsgebrauch gestattet. Die Kopiergebühren sind
abgegolten. Alle Rechte vorbehalten.

Textquellen: Katie Hoffman, Olathe, Kansas

16 Language: Save our water → (after Station 3)

Use the correct forms of the verbs in the box to complete the text. Sometimes more than one answer is possible.

> need to | should | be forced to | be supposed to | be required to | ought to | not have to | be said to

California's drought _____ be over for now, but it is still important to save water! In 2016 the average household water use per person was higher than in 2015. That's probably because the government restricted our water use before 2016. For example, people _____ wait 48 hours after it rained before they watered their gardens. I think it's sad that some people only save water when they _____. Yes, it's true that water use in agriculture is a much bigger problem. But people really _____ do their part for the environment and think about how they use water at home. If you don't know what changes to make, here are a few tips. While you're brushing your teeth, you _____ turn off the water. And you really _____ think about recycling the water you don't drink by giving it to your plants. In the past because of water conservation laws, some Californians _____ limit their showers to only five minutes or only fill half of the bath. That's a good tip even when there isn't a drought! If you don't think it's important, you _____ make these kinds of changes, but what will we do if one day there isn't any water left?

17 Language: Let's protect the environment → (after Station 3)

You want to write a blog similar to the one above to convince people to do more to protect the environment. Choose either the topic of air pollution or water pollution. Then use five of the verbs or expressions below to make sentences about what people can do to improve the problem.

> need to | must | ought to | should | be expected to | be required to | be supposed to | be forced to | be said to | have to

1. _____

2. _____

3. _____

4. _____

5. _____

Text smart 3   Argumentative texts

1   A letter to the editor

a) *Read the extract of an article on school leaving age. Note down the author's three main points.*

Harry Phibbs │ **Wednesday 7 January 2009**

A positive alternative would be to lower the school-leaving age back down to 14 but with the important condition that children are allowed to leave at this age only if they can pass an exam proving that they have achieved basic standards of English and Maths. This would have a life-changing effect. For children to be bored does not mean that they are stupid. The more bored a child is to be stuck at school, the greater the motivation to pass the exam. At Pimlico School, the comprehensive I went to, we used to call truancy[1] "bunking off[2]". The teachers were secretly pleased when the bored children "bunked off" because the alternative was them being in the lessons and disturbing them. Increasing[3] the school-leaving age will not cause the students to learn more – just more broken windows around the school. Children fed up with school need an escape route, not a longer sentence.

Source: www.theguardian.com (abridged and adapted)

1 **truancy** Schuleschwänzen │ 2 **bunk off (coll)** blaumachen │ 3 **increase** hier: erhöhen

b) *Analyse the structure and language of both letters to the editor. Say which letter is better and why.*

<table>
<tr>
<td>

A How right you are to say that a bored child is not necessarily a stupid one! However, your suggestion that it would be better for bored children to leave school at a younger age is total rubbish. Most children are bored at school *and* they would also be bored at work! Surely the answer to stopping boredom is to change the school day and school subjects. How many adults like to sit for hours on end and listen to somebody talking and then answer questions about it? It isn't because young people can't concentrate for long, as many researchers seem to say; it's because it isn't normal for humans to sit for so long and do the same things again and again. Another reason for students to be bored is because so much of what we learn at school is not relevant to our future lives. Who needs to be able to do higher maths? Why can more relevant subjects not be taught? Computers are used in almost every branch of industry and higher education, but how much are they used at school? Hardly at all! Most young people love to use computers or technical devices. School work could be made much more fun!

</td>
<td>

B I would like to thank Harry Phibbs for his excellent article published on 7 January. He has successfully summed up the situation for many students and teachers in schools and additionally made a sensible suggestion for a solution to the problem.

In my opinion the government wants to keep students at school longer to save money and to keep their unemployment figures down. The numbers of students who leave school and cannot find a job is continually very high. By keeping them in school, the government looks as though it is getting the country back to work. It is obvious, however, that students who have not done well after 11 years at school will not have done well after 13 years.

In conclusion, I am convinced that Phibbs' suggestion to lower the school-leaving age is the right one. Of course, this means that the job-training system in Britain will also have to change. I believe that Britain should follow Germany's example and support companies that train and pay students. In this way, the schools, the teachers and the students themselves can all benefit.

</td>
</tr>
</table>

c) *Write your own letter to the editor about this article. Use your notes from a).*

Green Line 5
Vorschläge zur Leistungsmessung
ISBN: 978-3-12-834254-2

© Ernst Klett Verlag GmbH, Stuttgart 2018 | www.klett.de
Von dieser Druckvorlage ist die Vervielfältigung für den eigenen
Unterrichtsgebrauch gestattet. Die Kopiergebühren sind
abgegolten. Alle Rechte vorbehalten.

Textquellen: Pauline Ashworth, Stuttgart; *Let them leave school at 14* by
Harry Phibbs, The Guardian, January 7, 2009

2   An argumentative essay

a) *Read the extract from an article in the Daily Mail. Decide if it is a persuasive essay or a neutral essay and explain why.*

Abigail Chandler │ Friday 3 November 2017

In some parts of the United Kingdom, 16 and 17-year-olds can already vote – such as in Scottish parliament and local elections. MPs will now debate on whether they should be allowed to vote in a general election – and it's about time.

There seems something immoral[1] about allowing young people to work, pay tax and risk their lives
5 for their country by joining the army, but to give them no say in how our country is run. They can contribute to the economy but have no say in how their taxes are used. They're trusted to drive heavy and potentially deadly vehicles[2] from the age of 17 but couldn't be trusted in a ballot box[3]. 16 and 17-year-olds are smarter and more capable[4] than most people think. Sure, your life experience is rather limited at 16, and there are big differences in maturity[5] levels from person to
10 person but plenty of 16-year-olds would be conscientious[6] voters. And the ones who have no interest in politics – well, like in every age group, they probably just won't bother[7] voting.
18 to 24-year-olds traditionally have the lowest voting turn-out of any age group, so the chances are that the number of 16 and 17-year-olds voting would be quite low too. The ones who would show up[8] to vote are the ones who have an opinion on who should be running the country. Maybe that
15 opinion will be informed by research, or by their family's typical voting habits, or by what they've seen on social media, or by simply choosing what they see as the least worst option[9] – in other words, exactly how everyone else chooses who they vote for.
A lower voting age would also mean that schools would have a good reason to start teaching the basics of politics. If their pupils will be allowed to vote, then schools should have a responsibility to
20 start teaching them about the British political system, or running debates in which pupils represent the different political parties. That would result in well-prepared 16-year-olds, who will go on to be more politically-engaged adults.
These young people are the ones who will have to live with the consequences of political decisions for longer than any other demographic[10], and they should be given the option of having a say. And
25 no, you can't ban a demographic from voting just because you think they'll vote 'incorrectly' (the opposite of whatever you believe in). I don't care whether a 16-year-old votes differently to me. I don't care if they can't be bothered to vote. I just care that they're at least given the chance.

Source: www.metro.co.uk (abridged and adapted)

1 **immoral** unmoralisch │ 2 **potentially deadly vehicles** potenziell tödliche Fahrzeuge │
3 **ballot box** Wahlurne │ 4 **capable** fähig │ 5 **maturity** Reife │ 6 **conscientious** gewissenhaft │
7 **not bother with sth** sich nicht mit etw. abgeben │ 8 **show up** auftauchen │
9 **least worst option** geringstes Übel │ 10 **demographic** Bevölkerungsschicht

b) *Analyse the language and structure of the essay and explain why it is or isn't well-written. Give examples from the text to support your opinion.*

c) *Choose one of the controversial topics below and write an argumentative essay for or against the issue.*

> Germany's education system is outdated and favours the children of educated parents.

> Alcohol should be banned in public places, just like cigarettes are.

> From the age of 16, students should be able to decide which subjects they want to continue studying.

Textquellen: Pauline Ashworth, Stuttgart; *The voting age SHOULD be
lowered to 16 – and this is why* by Abigail Chandler, Metro News,
November 3, 2017

Unit 1   G'day Australia!

Allgemeine Hinweise zur Bewertung von offenen Schreibaufgaben

Die insgesamt zu vergebende Punktzahl für offene Schreibaufgaben setzt sich aus den Bereichen inhaltliche Leistung (Orientierung an der Aufgabenstellung, Umfang, Textsorte, Textaufbau) und sprachliche Leistung (Sprache, Wortschatz, Strukturen, Orthographie) zusammen.

Allgemeine Hinweise zur Bewertung von offenen Sprachmittlungsaufgaben

Die insgesamt zu vergebende Punktzahl für offene Sprachmittlungsaufgaben setzt sich aus den Bereichen inhaltliche Leistung (Orientierung an der Aufgabenstellung / Bezug auf situativen Kontext, sinngemäße sowie situations- und adressatenbezogene Wiedergabe der Informationen) und sprachliche Leistung (eigenständige Formulierung, Wortschatz, Satzbau, Strukturen, Orthographie) zusammen.

1   Listening: Survival training (→ 12 Punkte)

1. She sees a spider.   2. kill the spider   3. He throws it out of the car.   4. call an ambulance   5. thousands of people   6. only one from spiders and a couple per year from snakes   7. It's not very comforting.   8. walk in the bush   9. They are going to find it.   10. Emily for a week, Jake for five days   11. in the outback   12. 18 days

2   Listening: A big hole (→ 11 Punkte)

1. b   2. b   3. a; b   4. a   5. c   6. c   7. a; c   8. b   9. c

3   Reading: A newspaper article

Comprehension (→ 13 Punkte)

1. between 65,000 and 80,000 years old   2. Aboriginal/indigenous people   3. They prove that Aborigines had lived in Australia much longer than was thought before.   4. in the journal *Nature*   5. because the native Australians had originally come from Africa   6. They prove that his people have been living there for a very long time.   7. the Mirarr people   8. It will be returned to the Mirarr people (at the end of the project).   9. people clearing out trees; mining   10. protect their land for the younger generations; stay on their own land forever; teach their kids about their people

Comprehension – Analysis – Evaluation (→ 35 Punkte)

a) (→ 5 Punkte inhaltliche Leistung)

Erwartungshorizont:
- About 11,000 Aboriginal artefacts have been found in Kakadu national park.
- They are between 65,000 and 80,000 years old.
- This proves that Aborigines have inhabited the area for at least 65,000 years (not 47,000 to 60,000 years as estimated before).
- This shows that they must also have left Africa and travelled to Australia much longer ago than previously thought.
- The site is on the traditional land of the Mirarr people. They have the total control over the dig and veto power and artefacts must be given back to them after the dig.

b) (→ 10 Punkte inhaltliche Leistung)

Erwartungshorizont:
- The indigenous people are proud that they have been living in Australia for much longer than estimated (l. 15: "We'd like to tell people we were here long enough").
- They are proud of their long culture (ll 15-16: "tell all the Balanda about the stories").
- The indigenous people have been given control over their land by the government for the first time (ll 17-19: "Under the agreement [...] at the end of the project.").
- They are proud and have new confidence now that they have a say about what is happening on their land (l. 20: "They have to bring it back here, it belongs to this place.").
- They accept that the white people dig up the artefacts (l. 21: "We trust them to work this place.").
- They want to preserve their culture and are afraid that white people might destroy their land (ll 22-23: "the country had to be protected [...] clearing out trees and mining").
- They feel that it is their land; they are connected to it and want to stay there and pass on their culture (ll 24-25: "We'd like to stay [...] who gave us the stories.").

Green Line 5
Vorschläge zur Leistungsmessung
ISBN: 978-3-12-834254-2

c) (→ 10 Punkte inhaltliche Leistung)
Individuelle S-Antworten

Inhaltliche Leistung:	→ 25 Punkte
Sprachliche Leistung:	→ 10 Punkte
Gesamtpunktzahl:	→ 35 Punkte

4 Reading: Angela

Comprehension (→ 12 Punkte)
1. true (ll 2-3) 2. false (ll 15-16) 3. true (ll 19-21) 4. false (l. 22) 5. false (ll 23-27) 6. true (ll 29-30)
7. false (ll 31-33) 8. true (ll 41-43) 9. true (ll 44-46) 10. true (ll 48-51) 11. false (ll 52-53) 12. false (ll 55-57)

Comprehension – Analysis – Evaluation (→ 35 Punkte)
a) (→ 5 Punkte inhaltliche Leistung)
Erwartungshorizont:

– Shirley asked Gracey to move in with them because it would be helpful to have an extra person to share the rent.
– Gracey wants to be around other black people. They have made university life easier for her.
– She feels at home around the other Murri girls because they have had the same experiences she has.
– Shirley and the other girls understand what it is like to be treated differently by white people.
– Now that Gracey has met other Murri girls, she doesn't feel alone anymore.

b) (→ 10 Punkte inhaltliche Leistung)
Erwartungshorizont:

– Angela is a white Australian girl who lives with her parents. She has just started university. She has always lived with people who are like her and has never experienced what it is like to live with people who are different from her.
– Gracey is an Aboriginal girl who lives with Angela at her parents' house. She has also just started going to university. She is used to living with white people and until recently didn't know how it is to be with other Aborigines.
– Gracey and Angela have been best friends for a long time (ll 1-2: "… were going to be best friends forever …").
– Since they started university, their relationship has changed. Gracey has met some other Aboriginal students and now being among people who are like her has become more important (ll 3-4: "… Gracey's Aboriginal heritage started to develop a new meaning.").
– Gracey wants to move out so she can live with the other Murri girls, but she is scared of telling Angela about it because she doesn't want to hurt her feelings (ll 20-21: "… took a quick look at my face … to guess.").
– Angela's and Cheryl's opinion are still important for her and she wants to consider their feelings (ll. 29-30: "If you want me to, I'll say no."; ll. 37-38: "… I wanted to talk it through with you and Cheryl.").
– When Gracey finally tells Angela that she wants to move out, Angela is very surprised and also hurt (l. 23: "I nearly drove us in the river."; ll. 35-36: "… too stunned to work out what I really thought.").
– Angela hadn't realized that Gracey has changed since she met the other girls. She thought they were still best friends and that Gracey was happy to be living with her (l. 19: "Still I didn't suspect"; ll 39-40: "I thought you were happy living with us. You know, sisters.").
– Now that Gracey has met people who are like her, she wants to be around them because they understand her. She thinks that Angela can't understand this because she has never had to try to fit in with people who are different from her (ll 43-47: "It's probably hard for you to understand … my skin colour.").
– Angela wasn't aware that Gracey still felt the effects of discrimination (ll 52-53: "I thought … anymore.").
– When Gracey met other Aboriginal people, for the first time she noticed that she had felt alone before. She has now realized that living with white people doesn't make her happy (ll 55-57: "Trouble is … not alone anymore.").

c) (→ 10 Punkte inhaltliche Leistung)
Individuelle S-Antworten

Inhaltliche Leistung:	→ 25 Punkte
Sprachliche Leistung:	→ 10 Punkte
Gesamtpunktzahl:	→ 35 Punkte

5   Writing: A report about your exchange program (→ 10 Punkte)

Lösungsvorschlag:

While most of my friends were still buying their presents last 22nd December, I was on my way to Australia! I and two other students were travelling to Sydney to take part in the GOAUSSIE exchange program. It's a very long flight to Sydney (about 20 hours), so we were glad when we arrived on 24th December, Christmas Eve! Once we were at the youth hostel, we could relax, but not for long. Our tour guide took us on a tour of Sydney Harbour, where we ate delicious food and took lots of great pictures. Normally we have snow and cold weather for Christmas, but not here in Sydney!
On 25th December we were all at a Christmas Party on Bondi Beach. Santa Claus was even there on a surfboard! On 27th December we explored Sydney Opera House, Sydney Harbour Bridge, the Museum of Sydney, and many more sights. The places were all so interesting that it would be impossible to say which one was my favourite. The highlight of my trip was the week that we spent in the outback (28th – 4th January). We took great walking tours through the landscape and learned lots about the indigenous animals. My favourite is the kangaroo. And we were able to talk to some Aborigines, who told us fascinating stories. They also told us what happened to the Stolen Generation, the children who were taken away from their parents and forced to grow up with white people. It was very interesting but very sad. For the next five days (5th – 10th January) we visited a school in Sydney and made lots of new friends. We also held a presentation about school life in Germany, and our new friends asked lots of questions! On 11th January we started the long trip home. One thing is certain: We all want to go back to Australia again!

Inhaltliche Leistung:	→ 6 Punkte
Sprachliche Leistung:	→ 4 Punkte
Gesamtpunktzahl:	→ 10 Punkte

6   Writing: A radio news report (→ 10 Punkte)

Lösungsvorschlag:

Bill: Good morning to our listeners and welcome to *All the News*. Today our reporter, Betty Smith, is speaking with Mary Jones about the plane crash that she and her husband survived. Over to you, Betty.

Betty: Yes, thank you, Bill. Mary and her husband, Greg, started off on a short outback tour with their plane to enjoy the beautiful landscape, just like they had done many times before. What happened this time, Mary?

Mary: Well, when we went to our plane in the morning, everything seemed normal. The sky was clear, the wind was good and my husband had already chosen the route that we would fly. We both were excited about our tour!

Betty: And how did the problems start?

Mary: Well, we had been flying for about 15 minutes when suddenly my husband had terrible pains in his chest. Then he couldn't get enough air and he couldn't control the plane any longer. I called an emergency number for help, but then the plane started to go down – it was terrible! Then we crashed. It was incredible, but I wasn't even badly hurt. However, my husband had a broken leg in addition to his chest pains and breathing problems. Luckily the emergency people had traced where we were in the air and could figure out where we might hit the ground. They found us very quickly.

Betty: What a scary experience! We're all very thankful for the great emergency help that got to you so fast. And we're even more thankful that you and your husband survived! Our best wishes to you!

Inhaltliche Leistung:	→ 6 Punkte
Sprachliche Leistung:	→ 4 Punkte
Gesamtpunktzahl:	→ 10 Punkte

7   Mediation: Travelling in Australia (→ 10 Punkte)

Lösungsvorschläge:

Hi James,
I can't wait to visit you in Sydney next month! I've had a look at a few websites and have found some interesting places we could visit together. First there's Noosa. Have you heard of it? It's about 120 km north of Brisbane. In Noosaville there are nice restaurants and cafés we could go to. The other part, Noosa Heads, has beaches which are great for surfing. I know how much you love surfing!
Another place we could visit is Agnes Water/1770, two neighbouring villages on the east coast. There aren't any exciting sights or party locations to go to, but apparently it's a great experience to drive along the coastline on a chopper and you can go surfing there, too. I think it's really more of a quiet place where you're not surrounded by tourists, like at the Great Barrier Reef.

Green Line 5
Vorschläge zur Leistungsmessung
ISBN: 978-3-12-834254-2

© Ernst Klett Verlag GmbH, Stuttgart 2018 | www.klett.de
Von dieser Druckvorlage ist die Vervielfältigung für den eigenen
Unterrichtsgebrauch gestattet. Die Kopiergebühren sind
abgegolten. Alle Rechte vorbehalten.

The Whitsunday Islands are very popular with tourists. The biggest one is Whitsunday Island, and Whitehaven Beach on the east coast is supposed to be very beautiful. How about going there? You can reach it by boat from Airlie Beach. From there you can also fly over the other islands by helicopter or water plane.
Tell me what you think. I look forward to hearing from you!

Hi Sienna,
I'm really looking forward to visiting you in Sydney soon! I've had a look at a few websites and have found some interesting places we could visit together. First there's Noosa. Have you heard of it? It's about 120 km north of Brisbane. There's a national park which is located along the coast. I know that you like spending time outside, so I thought you might enjoy visiting it. Australia Zoo isn't far away from Noosa either.
Another great place to enjoy nature is Lamington National Park in the southeast of Queensland. The largest subtropical jungle of Australia is located there. It stretches over more than 200 km^2 and you can see rainforests, ancient trees and more than 500 waterfalls.
We could also visit the Whitsunday Islands, a group of islands discovered by James Cook in 1770. The biggest one is Whitsunday Island. Whitehaven Beach on the east coast is supposed to be very beautiful. From May to September you might even be able to watch whales – wouldn't that be great? I know that you love animals!
Tell me what you think. I look forward to hearing from you!

Inhaltliche Leistung:	→ 7 Punkte
Sprachliche Leistung:	→ 3 Punkte
Gesamtpunktzahl:	→ 10 Punkte

8 Vocabulary: Safety in the outback (→ 8 Punkte)

1. on your own 2. likely 3. deadly 4. satellite 5. disturb 6. safety 7. litter 8. pick

9 Vocabulary: My family (→ 6 Punkte)

1. occupation 2. diversity 3. overseas 4. pretty 5. repair 6. relatives

10 Vocabulary: Australia Day (→ 7 Punkte)

protest; disrespectful; nomads; convicts; knowledge; childhood; anniversary

11 Language: Invitations (→ 8 Punkte)

Have you been invited; 'd just been asked; was given; Will … be held; is always organised; 's going to be shown; was … bitten; will … be protected

12 Language: Taronga Zoo (→ 9 Punkte)

Taronga is Sydney's city zoo, and as it was built at the harbour, it lives up to its name, Taronga, …
The location had been suggested by Albert Le Souef (because there was lots of space for the animals there).
One hundred years later wildlife is still protected by the zoo for future generations.
Today over 4,000 animals can be seen at the zoo.
These are the smallest species of penguin and they must be protected as they are in danger of extinction.
As they live near the city centre, these penguins are often attacked by dogs.
When possible these penguins are treated until they are healthy again and then they are set free in the wild.
The zoo can be reached by ferry within 12 minutes from the city centre.

13 Language: New Year now and then (→ 9 Punkte)

My friends and I got there early the first morning, so a few decorations were still being hung up and some other last minute preparations were being done.
I was surprised by all the different kinds of things that were being sold.
While we were being shown some special kitchen knives, one of my friends went to get us all her favourite Christmas food.
All around me all sorts of traditional Christmas songs are being performed by children and adults.
Sweet nuts are being eaten and Christmas punch is being drunk.
The skates are still being given to them and they are being told to be careful.

14 Language: January on the beach (→ 6 Punkte)

Sarah is having her hair cut.
Peter's parents have allowed him to / let him stay another week.
The lifeguard made Fiona clean up the litter.
Lizzie's mum let Lizzie go / allowed Lizzie to go surfing.
Lizzie's mum made her wear her T-shirt.
Pamela wants to have her photo taken with a famous surfer.

15 Language: An exchange trip to Sydney (→ 6 Punkte)

1. The students were offered a trip to Sydney (by the English teachers).
2. We were sent letters about our Australian partners and their families.
3. We were shown Sydney (by the families) when we arrived there.
4. I was taught some surfing tricks (by my new friend).
5. Jacob was given a new surfboard (by his host family).
6. We had been promised a great experience (by the teachers) before we left home.

16 Language: Car problems in the outback! (→ 5 Punkte)

If Dad had lent me his car, it wouldn't have broken down.
We could call / would be able to call someone if our mobiles worked.
If we don't find / go and look for water soon, we'll die of thirst.
If we left the car, nobody would find us again.
If we had stayed on the road, somebody would have found us.

17 Language: Moving to the outback (→ 8 Punkte)

used to go; didn't use to worry/think; used to buy; didn't use to think/worry; used to walk; used to meet; didn't use to have; used to be

Text smart 1   A short film

1 The plot (→ 8 Punkte)

1. He is running away.   2. "This is the police."; "Put your hands in the air."   3. He was running away because he was being chased.   4. His friend Maya is missing and he was the last person she phoned.   5. He is confused/worried.
6. He gets a phone call from a stranger who tells him to meet him.   7. 12 o'clock at Darley Road

2 Getting from picture A to picture B (→ 3 Punkte)

b) (You can hear the punch in the film.)

3 The setting (→ 4 Punkte)

Lösungsvorschlag:

The film starts at night-time on some stairs near a bridge. The city is probably London. The rest of the film clip takes place at a police station, mainly in an interrogation room. Both settings are very dark. There are no windows in the police station and the walls look old and dirty. It's an unpleasant place.

4 The genre and its key elements (→ 7 Punkte)

Lösungsvorschlag:

The genre is crime (or it could be film noir); it's a detective story. Key elements: darkness, night-time, running / somebody being chased, suspenseful music, the sound of a police car siren, police officers / detectives, a missing person, a crime has happened, a suspect, an object that makes somebody seem suspicious (mobile phone), a large map on a wall

Green Line 5
Vorschläge zur Leistungsmessung
ISBN: 978-3-12-834254-2

5 Body language and facial expressions (→ 8 Punkte)

Lösungsvorschlag:

A The detective / police officer is sitting very upright and has her eyes wide open. She is saying something to Greg. She seems annoyed and wants Greg to tell her the truth.

B Greg is leaning towards the two detectives / police officers. He can't believe they think he has done something wrong and he's also nervous, confused, maybe even a little scared.

C The detective / police officer is listening carefully to what Greg is saying and he's looking at him very closely. He looks very serious and sceptical. He is not sure if Greg is lying or telling the truth.

D Greg's eyes are very narrow, his mouth is shut. He is concentrating very hard and thinking of a way to escape from the police station.

6 Shot sizes (→ 6 Punkte)

Lösungsvorschlag:

A Here, a close-up shot (an extreme close-up shot) was used to show that Greg is thinking very hard. There's an idea forming in his head.

B Here, a (very) wide shot was chosen to show where Greg is. He wants to sneak out of the police station, so the viewer needs to know what the surroundings are like. Is there a way to escape?

Unit 2   The good life?

1 Listening: An unusual life (→ 12 Punkte)

1. a   2. c   3. c   4. b, c   5. a, b   6. a   7. a   8. b   9. c   10. a

2 Listening: Can I really do that job? (→ 11 Punkte)

	Jim	Chloe
What was the profession of the visitor who spoke to Jim/Chloe's group?	(ballet) dancer	firefighter
What did Jim/Chloe think about the profession before they heard the talk?	that it would be boring	that a woman isn't physically strong enough to do the job
What did Jim/Chloe learn about the jobs? Name 2 things for Jim and 3 things for Chloe.	1. you need to be very strong 2. it is good for your physical fitness	1. you have to do a lot of training / do difficult tests 2. you need to be able to work in a team 3. you have to be brave
Will Jim/Chloe consider doing the profession? Why/Why not?	No – he's not sporty enough	not sure / she will consider jobs that are usually thought of as men's jobs

3 Reading: About a boy

Comprehension – Analysis – Evaluation (→ 35 Punkte)

a) (→ 5 Punkte inhaltliche Leistung)

Erwartungshorizont:

– Will Freeman is 36 years old. He is single and doesn't have children. He doesn't have to work because his father wrote a popular Christmas song which made the family rich.

– Will doesn't have any close relationships or people he can rely on in an emergency, but this is OK for him. He knows people he can go out with for a drink or a meal or people he can a play a game of pool with in the evenings.

– For Will, it's a challenge to find different things to do during the day because the people he knows who he could do things with either have jobs or children – and he doesn't want to hang out with parents anyway.

– He divides his days into units of 30 minutes. He is proud of the way he manages to fill his days.

– He has managed his daily routine so well that he doesn't understand how people with jobs manage their lives.

b) (→ 10 Punkte inhaltliche Leistung)
Erwartungshorizont:

– The writer describes spending time as a challenge that Will has to face (e.g. ll. 19-20: "Whole hours, he found, were more intimidating.").
– The writer uses the metaphor of water to describe Will's way of dealing with time (ll 6-7: "huge ocean of time"; ll 7-8: "might have gone under and drowned").
– Will's ability of spending (or even wasting) time without actually having things to do is presented as a big achievement he is proud of (ll 7-8: "a less resourceful man … gone under and drowned").
– Even though Will doesn't have a job, he has developed a system which allows him to spend his days in an effective way. His system is presented in a way that makes filling days almost sound like a job (ll 18-19: "think of activities as units of time, each unit consisting of about thirty minutes"; ll 22-23: "nine units of a twenty unit day").
– Because Will regards even small everyday activities as tasks, he is surprised how other people can manage life and a job at the same time (ll 24-25: "he wondered how his friends … on the same day").

c) (→ 10 Punkte inhaltliche Leistung)
Individuelle S-Antworten

Inhaltliche Leistung:	→ 25 Punkte
Sprachliche Leistung:	→ 10 Punkte
Gesamtpunktzahl:	→ 35 Punkte

Comprehension (→ 13 Punkte)
a) (→ 7 Punkte)
1. c   2. b, c   3. b   4. b   5. c   6. b

b) (→ 6 Punkte)
1. true (ll 5-7: "Filling days […] at his disposal")   2. false (ll 9-11: "The evenings […] along the way")   3. true (ll 13-14: "They wouldn't be […] a broken heart")   4. true (ll 16-17: "all of these people […] paternity leave")   5. false (ll 18-19: "His way of dealing […] thirty minutes")   6. true (ll 23-25: "he had reached […] on the same day")

4   Reading: How to write a successful CV

Comprehension – Analysis – Evaluation (→ 35 Punkte)
a) (→ 5 Punkte inhaltliche Leistung)
Erwartungshorizont (mindestens 5 Dinge):

– Correct spelling and grammar are important, so check your CV for mistakes.
– The CV must include the skills and requirements the job advertisement asks for.
– Your CV should be easy to read (simple format and font) and not too long.
– Don't send a general CV, but write one which is specific to the job you apply for.
– All necessary pieces of information must be included (name, address, …).
– A good CV should show achievements, but not exaggerate.

b) (→ 10 Punkte inhaltliche Leistung)
Erwartungshorizont:

– At the beginning of the article the writer mentions how many applicants there are for most jobs (ll 1-2: "Employers receive … for every skilled job."). This way the reader becomes immediately aware of the importance of a good CV.
– The writer gets the reader's attention by addressing him/her directly (e.g. "Don't repeat" (l. 6); "your CV" (l. 8)).
– The writer gives a funny example to make the factual tone of the text more readable: ll 6-7: "Don't repeat the mistakes … interesting people".
– The tips from the expert are given in a well-structured list which makes them easy to read and understand (ll 14-25).
– The writer uses imperatives, which makes him sound more convincing (e.g. "Tailor" (l. 14); "Keep" (l. 16)).

c) (→ 10 Punkte inhaltliche Leistung)
Individuelle S-Antworten

Inhaltliche Leistung:	→ 25 Punkte
Sprachliche Leistung:	→ 10 Punkte
Gesamtpunktzahl:	→ 35 Punkte

Green Line 5
Vorschläge zur Leistungsmessung
ISBN: 978-3-12-834254-2

Comprehension (→ 18 Punkte)

a) (→ 5 Punkte)

1. because there are so many applicants for a job, you must present yourself well
2. include mandatory requirements, make sure the CV is relevant to the job
3. No, you should keep it simple and easy to read – two A4 pages are enough.
4. No, you don't, only if you apply for an acting or modelling job.
5. No, you should always be honest.

b) (→ 8 Punkte)

good:
– All the necessary personal details are included.
– The CV isn't too long.

bad/unnecessary:
– There is a spelling mistake (scool).
– The CV uses a very unusual font.
– The applicant doesn't list all the schools he went to (primary school is missing) and the years are missing.
– The applicant doesn't list any experience.
– The personal profile isn't related to the job description and uses colloquial language.
– The date of birth and photo are unnecessary.

c) (→ 5 Punkte)

Lösungsvorschlag:

Curriculum Vitae

Personal details:

Name:	Jamie Waldon
Address:	12 Beech Lane, Moseley, Birmingham B4 3LJ
Tel:	04937 8494737
E-mail:	jamwald@smail.co.uk
Date of birth:	19.10.2002

Education:

2006 – 2013:	St Agnes Primary School
2013 – (2018):	St Thomas Comprehensive School
Experience:	Lots of experience as waiter at friends' and family members' birthday parties

Personal profile:

I am looking for a job this summer because I want to do something useful and earn some money during the holidays. I am very sociable and energetic and I don't mind working hard. I like meeting new people and have good communication skills. I have a lot of experience of serving food and drinks to guests because I was a waiter at the birthday parties of many friends and family members. I am available most mornings and afternoons and am happy to travel to different locations.

---

5 Writing: An application letter (→ 10 Punkte)

Lösungsvorschlag:

Community Summer Work   28 Kingchester Road
Dovedale Road   Brighton BN1 35H
Faversham
Kent ME4 OGE

10th April 2018

Dear Mr Smith

Application for a position on the Community Summer Work Experience Project Program

I was happy to read your online advertisement calling for volunteers for positions with the Community Summer Work Experience Projects. I would like to apply for a position on your Seniors Work Project program.

I am 15 years old and am preparing for the GCSE exams later this year. Please see my CV (attached) for a complete record of my schoolwork. Although I work hard to get good marks, I also want to get practical work experience to find out which job(s) I might like to do in the future. For most of my life I lived in a neighbourhood where there were

 **Green Line 5**
Vorschläge zur Leistungsmessung
ISBN: 978-3-12-834254-2

© Ernst Klett Verlag GmbH, Stuttgart 2018 | www.klett.de
Von dieser Druckvorlage ist die Vervielfältigung für den eigenen
Unterrichtsgebrauch gestattet. Die Kopiergebühren sind
abgegolten. Alle Rechte vorbehalten.

57

several elderly people. I got to know them and I helped them with a variety of tasks. Last year I also helped with a few social activities at a local home for seniors. I enjoyed this experience very much, and I was told that I'm patient, I listen well and I'm very practical and creative. This is how I got the idea that I might like to find another job where I could work with the elderly. My family has just moved to a town here in the area and I've been hoping to find an opportunity here to get to know and help other elderly people. So I was very happy to find out about your Seniors Work Project!

I would be very grateful if you could consider my application for this program. My preference would be to work during the month of July. However, I could also work in August. I would also like to take part in the training days on 21st and 22nd June. I am available for an interview in the afternoon any weekday after 2 p.m. Thank you for your attention and I look forward to hearing from you soon.

Yours sincerely,

Jane White

Inhaltliche Leistung:	→ 6 Punkte
Sprachliche Leistung:	→ 4 Punkte
Gesamtpunktzahl:	→ 10 Punkte

6 Writing: A job description (→ 13 Punkte)

Lösungsvorschlag:

a) (→ 4 Punkte inhaltliche Leistung)
(flight attendant)
We are looking for responsible and motivated men and women with good people and team skills to join us as flight attendants. You can expect us to give you the best qualifications and job conditions: All of our employees are highly trained to deal with any situation on the ground or in the air, and the pay and benefits are good. And this is not an ordinary desk job, but one where you can meet many people and travel to different places all over the world. Does this sound like a job for you? Then please come to our training day on July 28, where you can fill out an application and talk to us. We look forward to meeting you!

(children's party organiser)
Do you enjoy fancy dress parties and creative party games? Do you enjoy being with children? Then being a children's party organizer could be the right job for you! In this position you are the contact person for parents who need help to organise their child's birthday or other type of party. You need to have good communication skills to find out what both parents and children want. It's always good if you're creative and can use this to make these ideas and wishes come true! You will also be expected to be at some parties and help with activities, so you should be practical and able to deal with unexpected situations (and lots of noise). A sense of humor is also good to have!

(a sport shop assistant)
Whether it's football or basketball, skateboarding or surfing, you love every sport. You've played or done many types, and you know lots about many more, right? If this sounds like you, then you might be the shop assistant we are looking for! Sally's Sports Centre is looking for someone who can help customers find exactly the right products that they need for the sport that they are interested in. Enthusiasm, excellent communication skills and a friendly personality are required: customers expect good advice about the products they need and how to use them. It's always good if you can tell them about your own experience if you play their sport. And everyone loves to talk about sports with another sports fan!

b) (→ 4 Punkte inhaltliche Leistung)

When I compare the job as children's party organiser and as a sport shop assistant, I would prefer to have the job as a party organiser. I'm not very good at playing a sport and I don't know very much about them. I can understand that other people are crazy about them, but I'm not, so I don't think that I could give the customers the attention and advice that they need. On the other hand, I am a very creative person, and I love parties and working with children. I already have lots of fun ideas for children's parties, as I've helped my mum to plan birthday parties for my little brother. The parties were always loud and sometimes they didn't go exactly like we had planned, but everyone always had a good time.

Inhaltliche Leistung:	→ 8 Punkte
Sprachliche Leistung:	→ 5 Punkte
Gesamtpunktzahl:	→ 13 Punkte

Green Line 5
Vorschläge zur Leistungsmessung
ISBN: 978-3-12-834254-2

7 Mediation: Organising a Fair Trade Day (→ 10 Punkte)

Lösungsvorschlag:

Hi! I asked my friend about the Fair Trade Day they organised. She said it was very successful. In general she said that it might be a good idea for you to look at the Fair Trade website because it has lots of suggestions and advice. Then she told me about the activities they did:

First they organised a Fair Trade breakfast: There were tables and displays in the school entrance hall so students could buy their breakfast as soon as they came in, and all the money they made went to Fair Trade. Their message was "Food for thought!" – they wanted the students to think about where their food comes from. They had posters that explained where and how most breakfast food is grown or produced, and how hard life is for farmers that produce the food. There were also some "good news" posters that showed how Fair Trade helps people by giving the farmers and producers fair pay, and educating and training them in new techniques. My friend told me that the day made them all really think about how easy our lives are compared to others in the world.

Another activity they did was a "Bake-Off" competition for teachers, parents and students. They baked small cakes and the rule was that they could only use Fair Trade ingredients. The judges (teachers, parents and students) tasted all the cakes and gave prizes to the winners. They also did a "taste test": Students tasted two cakes and had to guess which one contained Fair Trade products. This way, they wanted to show the students that Fair Trade products don't really taste different from "normal" products. Afterwards they ate all the cakes.

I hope these ideas will help you with your day. Good luck and let me know how it went!

Inhaltliche Leistung:	→ 7 Punkte
Sprachliche Leistung:	→ 3 Punkte
Gesamtpunktzahl:	→ 10 Punkte

8 Vocabulary: A Saturday job (→ 12 Punkte)

position; require; encourage; opportunity; people skills; hard-working; passionate; employees; attach; reference; applicants; experience

9 Vocabulary: Adjectives (→ 7 Punkte)

1. focused   2. adventurous   3. materialistic   4. desirable   5. fulfilling   6. realistic 7. passionate

10 Vocabulary: Using adjectives as nouns (→ 6 Punkte)

1. the homeless   2. the disabled   3. the rich   4. The elderly   5. the poor   6. The young

11 Vocabulary: Work activities (→ 8 Punkte)

1. providing   2. harvesting   3. stacking   4. dumping   5. carpenter   6. pay   7. listing   8. colleagues

12 Language: Improving the style of an application (→ 10 Punkte)

1. Therefore   2. However   3. Hopefully   4. Moreover   5. Of course   6. In fact   7. Of course   8. Unfortunately   9. Luckily   10. However

13 Language: A renovating project (→ 8 Punkte)

Lösungsvorschlag:

1. She saw a man painting a door.
2. She heard a baby crying.
3. She watched a woman planting flowers.
4. She saw a boy fall off a ladder.
5. She watched a girl cleaning windows.
6. She saw a girl drop her glasses.
7. She watched a man building a wall.
8. She noticed a dog jump over the wall.

14 Language: Present participle after verbs of rest and motion (→ 6 Punkte)

1. arrived feeling   2. stood waiting   3. ran along encouraging   4. caught myself thinking   5. stayed chatting
6. went home knowing

Green Line 5
Vorschläge zur Leistungsmessung
ISBN: 978-3-12-834254-2

© Ernst Klett Verlag GmbH, Stuttgart 2018 | www.klett.de
Von dieser Druckvorlage ist die Vervielfältigung für den eigenen
Unterrichtsgebrauch gestattet. Die Kopiergebühren sind
abgegolten. Alle Rechte vorbehalten.

59

15 Language: Inversion for emphasis (→ 6 Punkte)

1. Never before have I felt so nervous.
2. Hardly had I got out of bed when my phone rang.
3. Only then did I realise that I was already late.
4. No sooner had I arrived than the organiser came out to greet me.
5. Not only did I have to answer lots of questions, but I had to give a short presentation too!
6. Rarely have I been so happy!

16 Language: Non-defining relative clauses (→ 7 Punkte)

Alex Brodie, who is a 15-year-old inventor, has an important message for all teenagers. He says, "The world needs more young inventors!" His parents, who are both doctors, have always encouraged him to build and explore things and he reads anything he can find about science, which is his favourite subject. His older brother, who is at university, is very interested in world issues, which Alex enjoys discussing with him. At the moment he is working on some small building tools, which could help people in poorer countries. He also posts regular invention videos, which offer advice to other young inventors, online.

17 Language: Defining or non-defining clauses? (→ 10 Punkte)

Last Friday, my class had a work experience day that was really interesting. I was in the group who wanted to work with animals and we were sent to the office of an organisation which collects food, beds and toys for homeless dogs. First, the students, who had all arrived ready for a busy day, packed boxes. Then, we loaded them onto the organisation truck, which was waiting outside, and drove off to deliver them. It was a day which taught us a lot about teamwork. The people who worked at the shelters were very friendly – and we met some wonderful dogs, who we wanted to take home with us!

18 Language: *Do/does/did* for emphasis (→ 7 Punkte)

did; does; did; do; does; does; did

Text smart 2   Informative texts

1 Social media is harming the mental health of teenagers. The state has to act (→ 12 Punkte)

Erwartungshorizont:

Text **A** is a summary.

Good points: – It has an umbrella sentence.
– It has a clear structure and is written in a formal register.
– The text uses key terms from the original text.
Bad points: – The author uses direct speech.
– The wrong tense is used (simple past instead of simple present).

Text **B** is an analysis.

Good points: – The text uses a formal register.
– It examines particular aspects of the original text (intention, style, effectiveness).
– There are new paragraphs for new ideas, the main part and the conclusion.
Bad points: – The author gives a personal opinion.
– There is no introduction.

Green Line 5
Vorschläge zur Leistungsmessung
ISBN: 978-3-12-834254-2

© Ernst Klett Verlag GmbH, Stuttgart 2018 | www.klett.de
Von dieser Druckvorlage ist die Vervielfältigung für den eigenen
Unterrichtsgebrauch gestattet. Die Kopiergebühren sind
abgegolten. Alle Rechte vorbehalten.

2 A summary: Teenagers' IQ scores can rise or fall sharply during adolescence
(→ 12 Punkte)

Lösungsbeispiel:

In an online article by Ed Yong entitled 'Teenagers' IQ scores can rise or fall sharply during adolescence', which was published on www.theguardian.com on 19th October 2011, the author states that teenagers' IQs are not stable, but can change during teenage years. The author refers to a study and an expert from Oklahoma State University that both suggest that IQ scores can get better or worse during the teenage years.

The author then reports the details of the study that tested the IQ of 12- to -16 year-old pupils in two different years. The results showed that the average of the scores stayed the same, but that individual scores changed over the years. According to the author, the results challenge the general view that intelligence stays the same. As an example of this long-standing view he mentions the psychologists Alfred Binet and Jean Piaget, who both believed that mental development ended at the latest at 16.

Yong goes on to say that the study team wants to find out the reasons for the changes in IQ, and if these changes can also happen with adults. He concludes by quoting an article on the same topic in which the author states that the study gives hope to low achievers and a warning to those who believe that a high IQ will always stay high.

Inhaltliche Leistung:	→ 6 Punkte
Sprachliche Leistung:	→ 6 Punkte
Gesamtpunktzahl:	→ 12 Punkte

3 An Analysis (→ 12 Punkte)

Lösungsbeispiel:

The article by Ed Yong informs the reader about a study that has shown that teenagers' IQ scores can actually change over time and don't have to stay the same, as most people have believed.

First, the author presents the outcome of the study and contrasts it with the general view that the IQ scores of children won't change over time and can therefore be used to predict their future achievements. This contrast underlines the importance of the results of the new study.

Then, the writer provides the reader with the details of the study and quotes experts without giving his own opinion. This makes the information seem reliable and convincing. The author also uses objective language and important key terms to report the results of the study, without getting too scientific so that everybody can understand the results.

Overall, the author presents the reader with relevant and reliable information in an objective way. The article is easy to follow even for teenagers, which is important because the topic is especially relevant for them.

Inhaltliche Leistung:	→ 6 Punkte
Sprachliche Leistung:	→ 6 Punkte
Gesamtpunktzahl:	→ 12 Punkte

Unit 3   California dreaming

1 Listening: Historical events in Hollywood films (→ 11 Punkte)

1. said to be based on a true story / true events   2. make the films more dramatic or interesting   3. (black) baseball player   4. black player on his team   5. an adult woman; English explorer   6. a child   7. history through films
8. social issues / our country and its people / society   9. how people choose their government   10. tell a good story / entertain

2 Listening: Harvey Milk (→ 11 Punkte)

1. c   2. a   3. a; c   4. c   5. a; b   6. c   7. b   8. b; c

Green Line 5
Vorschläge zur Leistungsmessung
ISBN: 978-3-12-834254-2

© Ernst Klett Verlag GmbH, Stuttgart 2018 | www.klett.de
Von dieser Druckvorlage ist die Vervielfältigung für den eigenen
Unterrichtsgebrauch gestattet. Die Kopiergebühren sind
abgegolten. Alle Rechte vorbehalten.

61

3   Reading: The circuit

Comprehension – Analysis – Evaluation (→ 35 Punkte)

a) (→ 5 Punkte inhaltliche Leistung)
Erwartungshorizont:

- Francisco asks his older brother Roberto about his experiences at an American school.
- He feels anxious, but also excited about going to school for the first time.
- On his first day of school, he gets up early.
- He dresses in overalls and a flannel shirt.
- Although Roberto tells him that it's bad manners, he puts on a cap because he doesn't feel dressed without it.

b) (→ 10 Punkte inhaltliche Leistung)
Erwartungshorizont:

- Francisco is a boy who was born in Mexico. Together with his parents and his older brother Roberto, he travels to California to have a better life.
- The family moves from one place to the other to find work. This makes it difficult for Francisco to find friends.
- Francisco is about to have his first day at an American school.
- Francisco asks his brother Roberto about his experiences at an American school because he is the only one in the family who went to school. When Roberto tells him about his negative experiences, we can see that Francisco is very nervous and anxious about it from his reaction (l. 12: "I asked, rubbing my wrists").
- What Roberto tells him makes him feel scared about his first day (l. 16: "I wish I had not asked").
- Roberto has told him that his lack of English skills was a problem, so now Francisco is even more afraid because he doesn't speak English either (ll 17-18: "I did not speak … anxious."). Maybe Francisco was hoping for positive stories, but everything Roberto tells him makes him feel worse. Nevertheless, he is still excited about going to school.
- When Francisco dresses on his first day, he doesn't feel comfortable (l. 22: "I dressed in a pair of overalls, which I hated"). He puts on a cap even though his brother tells him it's bad manners. The cap reminds him of his father and it seems to give him a feeling of safety (ll 26-27: "I decided to wear it. Papá always … without it").

c) (→ 10 Punkte inhaltliche Leistung)
Individuelle S-Antworten

Inhaltliche Leistung: → 25 Punkte
Sprachliche Leistung: → 10 Punkte
Gesamtpunktzahl: → 35 Punkte

Comprehension (→ 14 Punkte)

a) (→ 5 Punkte)
1. false (l. 9: "hit on the wrists with a twelve-inch ruler"; l. 10: "angry tone")   2. false (l. 13: "guessed what the teacher wanted me to do")   3. false (l. 14: "some of the kids made fun of me")   4. true (l. 15: "had to repeat first grade")
5. true (l. 18: "excited about going to school")

b) (→ 9 Punkte)
1. Roberto's problems to understand things   2. go to school   3. what he said made him anxious about going to school   4. he doesn't understand English   5. a labor camp near Santa Maria   6. wear a cap to school; Roberto tells him it's bad manners; he doesn't feel dressed without it   7. moving around (to the same places) every season to find work on farms

4   Reading: California's Latest Trend: Forest Bathing

Comprehension – Analysis – Evaluation (→ 35 Punkte)

a) (→ 5 Punkte inhaltliche Leistung)
Erwartungshorizont:

- The new trend of forest bathing comes from Japan, where it has become a part of the country's medical system.
- The idea is to spend time in nature to have less stress, tension and anxiety. People have reported that they have fewer negative thoughts and their memory is better.
- Guides take groups of people to green areas throughout the state of California.
- A session lasts two to four hours, but is only one mile or less long.
- The aim is to experience nature through your senses. There is no destination.

Green Line 5
Vorschläge zur Leistungsmessung
ISBN: 978-3-12-834254-2

© Ernst Klett Verlag GmbH, Stuttgart 2018 | www.klett.de
Von dieser Druckvorlage ist die Vervielfältigung für den eigenen
Unterrichtsgebrauch gestattet. Die Kopiergebühren sind
abgegolten. Alle Rechte vorbehalten.

b) (→ 10 Punkte inhaltliche Leistung)
Erwartungshorizont:

– At the beginning of the article the author explains that Americans spend very little time outdoors and are stressed by their daily chores most of the time (ll 2-3: "working long hours … sitting at the computer"; ll 7-8: "and let's not forget that … driving to our destination").
– The author supports the statement that people spend lots of their time with stressful activities by giving lots of numbers (e.g. "87%", l. 2; "between five and seven hours", ll 3-4; "6% of our time", ll 7-8).
– At the end of the first paragraph, the author mentions how much money is spent on stress-related diseases (l. 10: "cost $125 to $190 billion a year"). → The whole first paragraph is filled with reasons that show why there is a need for relaxing activities.
– The next paragraph offers a solution for the problems: the new trend called forest bathing ("California's latest trend … may be the solution.", l. 11).
– The author supports this idea by reporting the positive effects of the trend (ll 13-15: "Research has shown … has also been shown to improve.").
– The last paragraph explains what forest bathing actually is and how it works. Here, the author addresses the reader directly ("But how, you might be wondering", l. 18; "experience your environment through your senses", ll 20-21; "You have to be willing to leave your cell phone at home!", l. 21). This creates the impression that he wants to interest the readers in trying out the trend.
– The last two sentences almost seem like an advertisement for forest bathing: "As we all know … in your area soon!", ll 22-23. Here it becomes clear that the author is convinced of the trend and suggests trying it out.

c) (→ 10 Punkte inhaltliche Leistung)
Individuelle S-Antworten

Inhaltliche Leistung:	→ 25 Punkte
Sprachliche Leistung:	→ 10 Punkte
Gesamtpunktzahl:	→ 35 Punkte

Comprehension (→ 16 Punkte)
a) (→ 10 Punkte)
1. They do not spend much time relaxing outdoors / work a lot / are busy most of the day.
2. use social media / play video games / participate in school or community activities
3. the practice of going out in nature to reduce stress / take a break / slow down
4. reduces stress / helps you to deal with stress better / less anxiety / fewer negative thoughts / stops you from thinking too much / memory improves
5. so you can experience the natural environment / so you take a break from normal activities
6. What California does first, other places in the US do afterwards.
7. no personal opinion / passive and active voice / humor at the end / the author directly addresses the reader

b) (→ 6 Punkte)
Lösungsvorschlag:

1. a new thing that lots of people want to try out   2. more and more; growing   3. an idea that something should be a certain way   4. to continue to happen   5. to be less active and relaxed   6. to be ready or happy to do something

5 Writing: A handout (→ 10 Punkte)

Lösungsvorschlag:

The world water shortage problem

1. General reasons for a water shortage
   a) The rising world population (9 billion by 2044)
   b) less than 3% fresh water on earth
   c) climate / weather conditions

2. California as a specific case
   a) water use for agriculture, food production, industry
   b) climate conditions
   c) problems caused by weather

Green Line 5
Vorschläge zur Leistungsmessung
ISBN: 978-3-12-834254-2

3. The result: problems on a local, national and global level:
   a) health (physical, emotional)
   b) economy (e.g. food shortages, higher prices)
   c) lifestyle (more time necessary for water-related problems, less for other things)

4. Conclusion: Water shortage is a serious global problem that must be dealt with now.

Sources: cartoonstock; *Green Line 5*, Ernst Klett Verlag

Inhaltliche Leistung:	→ 6 Punkte
Sprachliche Leistung:	→ 4 Punkte
Gesamtpunktzahl:	→ 10 Punkte

6   Writing: Interpreting diagrams (→ 13 Punkte)

a) (→ 4 Punkte inhaltliche Leistung)
Lösungsvorschlag:

From the pie chart it's clear that almost all of the water used in California is needed for agriculture or for the production of meat and milk products. Specifically, the fruits and vegetables that people eat result in 47% of how much water they use per day, and the meat and milk products that they eat for 46%. Four percent of the water that they use per day is used for the industrial products that they need (e.g. clothes), and just 3% of the total of the water that they use per day is for household use (e.g. toilet, cooking, shower).
According to the bar graph, on average each person in the US uses nearly about 8,000 litres of water a day, more than twice the amount of water each day that most other people in the world do. The water footprint of each Californian is higher than that of each person in Germany. Both the Californians and the Germans use more water per day than the average person in the world.

b) (→ 4 Punkte inhaltliche Leistung)
Lösungsvorschlag:

It's clear that Californians must produce the meat and milk products that they use and sell in new ways that don't require so much water. The same is true for the fruits and vegetables that they produce. Together, both of these aspects are responsible for 93% of peoples' water use, so these are the areas where people need to save the most water. It might help if people didn't eat so much meat, because then not so many cows, chickens, etc. that consume water would be needed. It would be great if an economical way were discovered in the future to make salt water into fresh water. This could solve water problems all over the world!

Inhaltliche Leistung:	→ 8 Punkte
Sprachliche Leistung:	→ 5 Punkte
Gesamtpunktzahl:	→ 13 Punkte

7   Mediation: Hollywood, here I come? (→ 10 Punkte)

Lösungsvorschlag:

Hi Brian,
I'm glad to hear that you like living in California. I think you're right – Hollywood is a fascinating place and I can understand that the idea of becoming an actor is exciting. But I really think that you should be careful and think about it realistically. I found an article in which experts say that the path to becoming an actor is long and often hard. There are lots of workshops and academies that promise they'll make you famous soon, but most of the time you just pay a lot of money for bad classes. So if anyone promises you a successful career very fast, you should be very sceptical, because that's an unrealistic promise! Experts from the film business say that if you are really interested in becoming a serious actor, you should go the traditional way and attend a good drama school for three to four years. They say that without a good education, the chances of making a living with your acting career are really bad. If you really decide to become an actor and finish drama school, there are special courses you can do afterwards. These can teach you specific techniques, like camera acting. But even if you do all this, there is no guarantee that you will be successful. It's a hard industry, especially since many film and TV producers are trying to save money in productions. In any case, I really think that you should finish school before you go to Hollywood. I don't mean to be too negative about your idea and I hope that you will be successful! I wish you the best of luck. Hope to hear from you again soon!

Inhaltliche Leistung:	→ 7 Punkte
Sprachliche Leistung:	→ 3 Punkte
Gesamtpunktzahl:	→ 10 Punkte

Green Line 5
Vorschläge zur Leistungsmessung
ISBN: 978-3-12-834254-2

8   Vocabulary: Character traits (→ 8 Punkte)

1. b   2. e   3. f   4. a   5. h   6. c   7. g   8. d

9   Vocabulary: Collocations (→ 8 Punkte)

1. shoot a film   2. sports craze   3. strong economy   4. start-up company; keep their head above water   5. try your luck; entertainment industry; chalk it up to experience

10   Vocabulary: Natural disasters (→ 10 Punkte)

damage; wildfires; floods; On average; slight; recorded history; emergency; coordinate; climate change; be expected

11   Language: Working at an internet start-up (→ 12 Punkte)

are you catching; leaves; are taking; Are you eating; 'm eating; 'm meeting; 're discussing; starts; ends; gets started; 'm not going; 're working

12   Language: Off to Hollywood (→ 6 Punkte)

1. You probably won't be living your dream right away.
2. You'll be going to one audition after another at the beginning.
3. You'll be waiting in line for hours with other people who also dream of becoming actors.
4. I'm sure your parents will be asking if you will come home soon.
5. You'll be entertaining people on the street to make money.
6. Film directors will be looking for 'extras' for their movies. That could be your lucky chance!

13   Language: One possible world (→ 6 Punkte)

1. By 2050, car companies will have produced cars that drive themselves.
2. By 2035, we will have cleaned up the oceans.
3. Hopefully, in 25 years countries will have ended wars.
4. But humans won't have found life on other planets.
5. And most of them still won't have stopped eating meat.
6. But scientists will have developed medicine to make people live longer.

14   Language: Sequoia National Park (→ 6 Punkte)

a; —; the; the; a; —; the; an; a; A; —; a

15   Language: Article or no article? (→ 10 Punkte)

1. the education; education   2. Competition; the competition   3. risk; the risk   4. Ability; the ability   5. the culture; culture

16   Language: Save our water (→ 8 Punkte)

is said to / is supposed to; were forced to / were required to; are forced to / are required to / need to / are supposed to; should / ought to; ought to / should; ought to / should; were forced to / were required to; don't have to

17   Language: Let's protect the environment (→ 5 Punkte)

Lösungsvorschlag:

1. To achieve less air pollution, more people should use electric cars.
2. Also, people need to use their cars less and walk or ride their bikes instead.
3. Public transport needs to become cheaper so more people use it.
4. Cities ought to create more parks because plants improve the air quality.
5. Companies have to think of ways to produce clean energy.

Text smart 3   Argumentative texts

1 A letter to the editor (→ 18 Punkte)

a) (→ 3 Punkte)
Erwartungshorizont:

– The school-leaving age should be lowered to 14.
– The condition should be that students pass an exam which proves they have a basic level of knowledge in English and Maths.
– Students who are bored (not stupid) would benefit from the possibility of leaving school sooner.

b) (→ 5 Punkte)
Erwartungshorizont:

– Letter **B** is a better example of a good letter to the editor:
– It uses a formal tone.
– The paragraphs are clearly structured. This makes the letter reader-friendly.
– Letter **A** uses colloquial language.
– The paragraphs aren't structured – this makes the letter less reader-friendly than letter **A**.

c) (→ 10 Punkte)
Individuelle S-Antworten

Inhaltliche Leistung:	→ 5 Punkte
Sprachliche Leistung:	→ 5 Punkte
Gesamtpunktzahl:	→ 10 Punkte

2 An argumentative essay (→ 20 Punkte)

a) (→ 2 Punkte)
Erwartungshorizont:

– The given text is an persuasive essay. The author gives her own view right at the beginning and presents arguments which support her view.

b) (→ 8 Punkte)
Erwartungshorizont:

– In general: The author uses rather informal and emotional language to argue her point:
  "and it's about time", l. 3; "well, like in every age group, they probably just won't bother voting", l. 11; "I don't care", l. 26/27 → This is not the formal choice of language an essay requires, so this text is not a good example of a formal and serious argumentative essay. However, the emotional language makes the essay convincing because it stresses how important the topic is for the author.
– The essay has a clear structure:
  – It starts with an introduction which presents the main point: 16- and 17-year olds should be allowed to vote in all parts of the UK (ll 1-3).
  – The main body presents arguments for and against the issue (ll 4-22). The structure of the arguments is pro-con-pro-con-pro → The author shows that she knows the different views on the issue.
  – The conclusion presents another argument for the writer's view. By presenting two pro arguments towards the end of her essay the author tries to convince the reader. The language used in the conclusion is very emotional.
– The author doesn't give quotations and only one objective fact (l. 12: "18 to 24-year-olds traditionally have the lowest voting turn-out of any age group"). → The essay tries to convince the reader of the writer's personal opinion in a rather subjective and emotional way.

c) (→ 10 Punkte)

Lösungsvorschlag „From the age of 16, students should be able to decide which subjects they want to continue studying":

Students today face a lot of pressure to get a good job and be successful later in life. Schools try to give students a wide variety of knowledge to help them have good chances of success. However, students often have to study subjects that are either uninteresting or difficult for them. The question is whether it would make sense to allow students to decide which subjects they want to continue studying from the age of 16.

Students often have to study subjects that are very difficult or just boring for them. Many are convinced that they will never need some of the things school teaches them in their later lives. If students were able to choose their subjects, it would allow them to focus on their interests and strengths and subjects they think are important for their future studies or career. For example, if a student is very good at Science and Maths and plans to become an engineer or IT manager, he or she would benefit from focusing on more scientific topics and fewer topics like RE or social studies.

Another point in favor of this idea is that teachers often have to spend a lot of time explaining things to students who aren't good at a subject or who aren't interested in learning about it. During this time, many students who are interested and motivated become bored. If the classes consisted of students who really want to learn the topics, teachers could teach them more effectively, and this would be a benefit for both the students and the teacher.

On the other hand, however, at the age of 16 students might not know yet which subjects they will need in later life. It could turn out that their interests change when they are older and they might regret not having learned certain things when they made an earlier decision about a career. Take a student, for instance, who was never interested in foreign languages at school, who decides to study medicine – once the student is at university, he or she might realize that it would have been an advantage to study Latin at school.

Secondly, there is the risk that some students don't think about their choice of subjects carefully at this age. Some might consider their future studies or careers, but many will probably do what is easiest and choose subjects that they are good at and drop subjects that are a challenge for them. However, this way of choosing might prevent students from learning things that are very important for their adult life.

To sum up, the question if students should be given more choice regarding the subjects they study is an interesting and important one, but there are many different things to consider before changing our school system.

(alternativer letzter Absatz für einen* persuasive essay*:)

There are arguments in favor of letting students decide which subjects to continue studying from the age of 16, but there are even stronger ones against it. Young people can't know all about their skills, interests and strengths at age 16 and they should have more time and opportunity to learn about them.

Inhaltliche Leistung:	→ 5 Punkte
Sprachliche Leistung:	→ 5 Punkte
Gesamtpunktzahl:	→ 10 Punkte

Green Line 5
Vorschläge zur Leistungsmessung
ISBN: 978-3-12-834254-2

© Ernst Klett Verlag GmbH, Stuttgart 2018 | www.klett.de
Von dieser Druckvorlage ist die Vervielfältigung für den eigenen
Unterrichtsgebrauch gestattet. Die Kopiergebühren sind
abgegolten. Alle Rechte vorbehalten.

67

Unit 1

Warm up:
- Are there any animals that you are afraid of? If so, which ones?
- Would you dare to touch a dangerous or even poisonous animal? Why / Why not?
- Have you ever been bitten or stung by an animal? Describe how it felt and how you reacted. Did you have to see a doctor? (If you haven't been bitten or stung, how do you think you would react?)
- Do you sometimes read news reports? What kind of reports are you most interested in?

Monologues: Model answers

A The picture shows a crocodile lying in the sand. Somebody is putting her/his hand in its mouth / between the sharp teeth.
Possible story:
- a trip to a crocodile farm
- the person was dared to do it by friends (as a test of courage)
- a holidaymaker wanted to take a cool picture
- a vet who was doing check-ups and was bitten

B In the picture you can see a big black spider that is crawling on somebody's hand or leg.
Possible story:
- a new species has been discovered
- the person was dared to do it by friends (as a test of courage)
- a holidaymaker wanted to take a cool picture
- some spiders aren't as dangerous as people think they are

Dialogues: Model answers

Partner A/B (Set 1)
A: I think the friends are responsible for the injuries because they forced the teenager to jump.
B: I'm sorry, but I don't agree. In my opinion, it's the teenager's fault because he could have said no. Moreover, real friends don't ask you to do things like that, and they would accept it if you say you won't do it.
A: That's true. I think he should look for new friends.
B: I agree. I also think that his "friends" should be punished for daring him to jump, don't you think?
A: Yes, you're right. From my point of view they should help people at a hospital or talk to kids at schools about what they did, and what they've learned.
B: Those are good ideas. Alternatively, they could do work for an animal project (e.g. that protects endangered species). …

Partner A/B (Set 2)
A: *individuelle Schülerlösungen*
B: *individuelle Schülerlösungen*
Possible questions:
Why did you put your hand in the crocodile's mouth?
Have you ever done anything before that was so dangerous?
How did you feel before you put your hand between its teeth, while doing it and after?
Were you aware that the crocodile might bite you and cause injury, and if yes, why did you take the risk?
Looking at the picture now, how does it make you feel?
Would you do it again?
What's the next challenge/risk you want to take?
After you were bitten, how long did you have to stay in hospital? / How long did the injury take to heal?
Can you use your hand the same way that you did before the injury?

Green Line 5
Vorschläge zur Leistungsmessung
ISBN: 978-3-12-834254-2

Text smart 1

Warm up:
- What kind of films do/don't you like?
- What's your favourite film? Why do you like it?
- What media do you use to watch films (e.g. streaming, cinema, DVD, TV)?
- How do you decide which film you want to watch (e.g. reviews, zapping, recommendation by friends)?

Monologues: Model answers

A In the still Greg is running up some stairs near a bridge because he's being chased. The scene is set at night-time and the city is probably London.

The music sounds rather scary, which helps the viewer to realize that something bad is about to happen.

A long shot is used at the beginning to establish who the main character is, to show how frightened Greg is (he's running fast) and to give the viewer information about the setting.

The scene is important for the clip because it sets the mood of the clip, and it shows how Greg is feeling.

B The scene takes place in an interrogation room at a police station. The room/setting is very dark, but there is one bright light hanging down from the ceiling. There are no windows in the police station and the walls look old and dirty. It's an unpleasant place.

Here a medium shot is used to show a small group of people in the interrogation room. The music is very quiet/in the background, so you can hear people talking. This helps to keep up the suspense.

The scene is important for the clip, as Greg gets to know that he's the prime suspect in a missing person case, and the missing person is his friend Maya.

Dialogues: Model answers

Partner A/B (Set 1)

In the discussion, students should mention the following as examples for the genre crime:
- The settings are dark and dimly lit. This creates a dark and mysterious atmosphere and underlines the mood.
- The atmosphere becomes even more scary because of an anonymous phone call, where Greg is told what to do "if he wants to see his friends alive again" (happens in many crime stories).
- Some typical details are included, for example an interrogation room, people wearing police uniforms, a big map, posters (of the missing person and the suspect). These create the typical setting of crime films.
- The body language used by the actors in the interrogation room are typical of people who are questioning / being questioned.
- Scary/exciting music is used to build up suspense.

Partner A/B (Set 2)

A: For the next part I'd choose option A because once the police officers notice that Greg has run away, they'll look for him as he's the prime suspect.

B: Sorry, but to me this doesn't make much sense. I think the next part should focus on finding Maya because that's what's most important for Greg.

A: I agree, so let's choose option B.

B: Yes, this way we can keep up the suspense for a little longer. The setting should continue to be dark.

A: And we could show the darker / more scary side of London.

B: That's true. Greg could call some friends and ask them to help him find Maya. And when morning/daylight comes, they find her and the music becomes more cheerful.

A: I like that idea. For the part at night we should use medium and close up shots.

B: Yes, that way we can show best what the characters are doing and feeling …

Green Line 5
Vorschläge zur Leistungsmessung
ISBN: 978-3-12-834254-2

© Ernst Klett Verlag GmbH, Stuttgart 2018 | www.klett.de
Von dieser Druckvorlage ist die Vervielfältigung für den eigenen
Unterrichtsgebrauch gestattet. Die Kopiergebühren sind
abgegolten. Alle Rechte vorbehalten.

69

Unit 2

Warm up:
- If you've had a job before, describe what you did and if you liked it or not.
- If you haven't worked before, what kind of job would you like to have, and why?

Monologues: Model answers

A

Teenage boy: My name is … . I'm 16 years old, and I'm still at school. I don't get much pocket money, so I want to earn some extra money to go to a summer camp. I'm into sports and like cool outfits. That's why I decided to apply for this position. I'm feeling a bit nervous now. I hope I won't be asked any weird questions.

Teenage girl: My name is … and I'm 16 years old. I'm still at school. I don't get much pocket money, so I want to earn some extra money to buy a new smartphone. I like nice clothes and I like dealing with people. I'm confident that I'll get the job because I've worked in a shop before.

Possible questions:
- How many hours will I be expected to work per week?
- How much will I get paid per hour/month?
- What exactly will I be required to do?

B

Teenage boy: My name is … . I'm 16 years old, and I'm still at school. I like animals and I want to become a vet. I think it's important to get some work experience and to find out whether I'd really like to work with animals for the rest of my life. I'm curious how the interview will go!

Teenage girl: My name is … . I'm 16 years old. I'm very interested in wild animals and what zoos are doing to help them. That's why I hope to get this job, but if I don't, I'll be happy that I gained experience with interview situations. Maybe it will also give me an idea about the job I'd like to have after my studies.

Possible questions:
- Are the working days the same each week?
- Will I be working together with someone?
- Will I be allowed to choose which of the animals I'll be taking care of?

Dialogues: Model answers

Partner A/B (Set 1)

Possible skills:

patient (work with children, the elderly and disabled), have good communication and people skills, be creative (think of new activities or events) and reliable, perhaps know a foreign language (deal with people with different backgrounds)

Possible questions:
- What skills can you bring to the job?
- Why do you think you would be a good addition to our team?
- When / How many days per week would you be available? Also on weekends?
- If your little brother or sister were bored, what would you do or say to him/her?
- When you visit your grandparents, what do you like to do together?
- What would be a good event / new activity to offer at the community centre?

Partner A/B (Set 2)

A: Excuse me, can I ask you a question?

B: Yes, sure. How can I help you?

A: I really like the clothes you sell. But why are they more expensive in your shop?

B: Well, you pay more for the products so the people who make them can have better lives.

A: And what exactly does that mean?

B: It means that our products are made in a fair and safe environment. The trousers you're holding weren't made by children, but adults. All of our employees' children go to school, and the employees earn fair wages.

A: And do they have proper housing?

B: Yes, they live in simple houses and have access to clean drinking water.

A: That's brilliant. I'm glad there are companies like yours! I'll definitely come back to your shop and happily pay more money for the things you offer.

Green Line 5
Vorschläge zur Leistungsmessung
ISBN: 978-3-12-834254-2

Unit 3

Warm up:
- Would you like to be rich and famous one day? Why / Why not?
- What are the things in life that make you happy?

Monologues: Model answers

A

The first quote says that fame and success are two very different things. Fame means that many people know you and talk about you; success means you have achieved a goal that you had chosen for yourself.

The second quote says that only money and fame don't make people happy. Nicki Minaj's happiness comes from having an optimistic or relaxed way of looking at / thinking about life.

Possible answers to what brings happiness to a famous person:
- more money and more power
- being able to buy anything
- helping others and the community
- having a good family life
- being healthy
- going to the cinema or a football match without being noticed by the crowd

B

The first quote says that fame can have negative effects. It might mean that once an actor gets famous, fame itself becomes more important than doing one's best. It might also refer to the negative aspects that come with fame, e.g. having no private life.

The second quote says that in the past, people became actors because they loved acting. Maggie Smith criticizes that today some people start a career in show business not because they love acting, but because they want fame.

Possible opinions:
- Loving what you do and doing your best should be in the foreground, not being famous. It's a waste of life not to do what you love!
- Fame is most important because it means that you are successful in your career. What good is it to love your job if you can't make a living with it or if you lose it?

Dialogues: Model answers

Partner A/B (Set 1)

A: I think I'd buy an island.
B: Why would you do that?
A: Well, I'm most happy when I'm in a warm and sunny place with no people around. I'd name the island after me. This way I'll be famous and be remembered.
B: I don't think that's a good idea. We've made a lot of money because people bought our product, and now it's time that we give something back to society.
A: What do you mean?
B: I'd spend the money on helping people in need, like the homeless. Some of them lost their homes because the company they used to work for closed down. We could offer them a new chance in life, perhaps pay for their training and help them to find a new home.
B: You're right. But I still think we deserve to go somewhere nice on holiday.

Partner A/B (Set 2)

Possible answers:
- politicians (e.g. Obama for establishing more widespread healthcare in the USA, Helmut Kohl who worked for a united Germany)
- musicians (like U2 who raised money for Africa), entrepreneurs or inventors (who do a lot to protect the environment)
- volunteers (who help people in need)
- artists (who start new art forms)
- sports figures (who help young people also interested in sports)
- movie stars (who acted in films about important social/historical events)

 Klett

Green Line 5
Vorschläge zur Leistungsmessung
ISBN: 978-3-12-834254-2

© Ernst Klett Verlag GmbH, Stuttgart 2018 | www.klett.de
Von dieser Druckvorlage ist die Vervielfältigung für den eigenen
Unterrichtsgebrauch gestattet. Die Kopiergebühren sind
abgegolten. Alle Rechte vorbehalten.

71

Bewertung der Sprachkompetenz						
Kriterien/deren Erfüllung	voll	nahezu	im Wesentlichen	teilweise	kaum	nicht
inhaltlich richtig						
inhaltlich vollständig/ausführlich						
sprachlich verständlich						
sprachlich korrekt						
phonetisch korrekt						
intonatorisch korrekt						
adressaten-/situationsgerecht						
selbstständig						

Green Line 5
Vorschläge zur Leistungsmessung
ISBN: 978-3-12-834254-2